PASSION

PASSION

Contemporary Writers
on the Story of Calvary

Edited by

OLIVER LARRY YARBROUGH

Maryknoll, New York 10545

ORBIS BOOKS
Maryknoll, New York 10545

Fathers and Brothers
MARYKNOLL.

Founded in 1970, Orbis Books endeavors to publish works that enlighten the mind, nourish the spirit, and challenge the conscience. The publishing arm of the Maryknoll Fathers and Brothers, Orbis seeks to explore the global dimensions of the Christian faith and mission, to invite dialogue with diverse cultures and religious traditions, and to serve the cause of reconciliation and peace. The books published reflect the views of their authors and do not represent the official position of the Maryknoll Society. To learn more about Maryknoll and Orbis Books, please visit our website at www. maryknollsociety.org.

Manufactured in the United States of America.

Manuscript editing and typesetting by Joan Weber Laflamme.

Bible versions used: The Introduction and Chapter 4, the New Revised Standard Version; Chapters 1 and 5, the King James; Chapter 5 also uses Cook's libretto for *The Passion of Jesus of Nazareth*; Chapter 2 references Richmond Lattimore, *The Four Gospels and the Revelation* (New York, 1979); Chapter 3, the New International Version.

Library of Congress Cataloging-in-Publication Data

Passion : contemporary writers on the story of Calvary / edited by Oliver Larry Yarbrough.
 pages cm
 Includes bibliographical references.
 ISBN 978-1-62698-119-5 (pbk.)
 1. Passion narratives (Gospels) 2. Jesus Christ—Passion. 3. Bible. Gospels—Criticism, interpretation, etc. 4. Catholic Church—Doctrines. I. Yarbrough, O. Larry, editor.
BT431.3.P36 2015
232.96—dc23

                                                    2014028549

Contents

Acknowledgments

I acknowledge and express my appreciation to the president and fellows of Middlebury College for supporting the production of this volume. Funds came from the Charles P. Scott Endowment and the Pardon Tillinghast Professorship. Charles and Pardon were colleagues in my early years at Middlebury; I remember them fondly.

Contributors are three colleagues, one former student, and a new friend. I thank four of them for giving the lectures that were to become essays in this volume and for their patience as it went through several stages of development. I am grateful to John Elder for later agreeing to write on Matthew specifically for this volume.

I thank another former student, Matthew Weinert-Stein, for his editorial assistance and for helping to secure permissions.

Introduction

"Let the reader understand"
—MARK 13:14

No story in the Gospels is as well known as the Passion, with the possible exception of the birth narratives in Matthew and Luke that inform both religious and popular versions of Christmas celebrations. But they are of a very different sort. The Passion Narrative, or elements of it, has been part of Christian worship from earliest records, as one of Paul's letters to the Corinthians indicates (1 Cor 11:17–34). It became part of the Holy Week observances in Jerusalem from as early as the third century—as reported by a prominent woman named Egeria, who took part in the observances while on pilgrimage to the biblical sites in what was already coming to be called the Holy Land. Since then, the Passion Narrative has been the theme of countless hymns, poems, musical compositions, paintings, sculptures, novels, dramas, and films. Scholars of all sorts have turned their attention to the Passion Narrative, analyzing every part of the story in meticulous detail. And it must never be forgotten that since gaining power following the "conversion" of Constantine, Christians have all too frequently used the Passion Narrative as a weapon to bludgeon Jews.

In this volume five writers tell the story again. The first four—John Elder, Julia Alvarez, Stephanie Saldaña, and Jay Parini—tell it with one of the Gospels as a starting point; the last—Elizabeth

Cook—tells it by weaving all four Gospels together. None found the telling easy, though each for different reasons. Some found it difficult to tell the story when forced to work with only one Gospel. They found it constraining; having grown up with the story, they knew there were other parts to it that their Gospel did not have. Having grown up with the story presented other challenges as well. All five of the writers refer (without being prompted) to memories of early experiences with the story; some wrestle with the challenge of what to do with it now, whether because of its content or the ways it has been used and abused. Elizabeth Cook faced some of the challenges of the other writers but had at least one peculiar to her own task: how to choose what to include and how to arrange the narrative. For her, finding a way to sort through the similarities and differences among the Gospels was especially challenging.

All five of the contributors to the volume are master storytellers in their own right. They have written novels, short stories, poems, screenplays, memoirs, and essays. Most are also master teachers. So they all come back to this story with an understanding of how to read a story—and how to tell a story. Reading their stories is a rich experience.

Like John, Julia, Stephanie, Jay, and Elizabeth, I also grew up with the story of Jesus' crucifixion, the Passion. I heard it every year on Palm Sunday; I listened to my family's recording of Handel's *Messiah*—Sir Thomas Beecham's lush 1959 performance with the Royal Philharmonic Orchestra; I saw it dramatized in numerous movies and once in a live tableau performed at the ancient Native American burial grounds in Moundville, Alabama. Unlike them, however, I did not become a writer but a biblical scholar. So, in many ways, my approach to the Passion is different from theirs, being shaped by the tools and methods biblical scholars bring to their reading of the text. Using these tools and methods also allows for rich experiences in reading the Passion—and other parts of the Bible. Teaching and working with students enriches it even more, whether the students already know the texts or are reading them for the first time.

When I teach the Gospels, I commonly begin with Mark, asking students to read it through in one sitting. I also ask them to make two lists in preparation for discussing the assignment. One list is to include the parts of the story that surprise them; the other list is to include the parts of the story they were surprised not to find. The lists vary, of course, depending on how familiar any individual student already is with the story. If there is a pattern in the lists, it is that students who know the Bible least see things that those who know it best often miss—though the students who have a general knowledge of the Bible can also be surprised with what they find (or don't find) when they read a single Gospel all the way through. It is always intriguing to read the lists and to work with the students as we create a common list in discussions. The lists we put together as a group are wide ranging and, almost invariably, include most of the important themes and issues that appear in the history of Marcan scholarship. In identifying the main questions, the students take their first steps in learning how to seek answers to them. And thus we begin our study together.

From year to year the lists of surprises in Mark include any number of things Jesus says and does, like cursing a fig tree (11:12–26), telling people he heals not to say anything about him (which happens throughout the Gospel), refusing to heal the Syro-Phoenician woman's daughter (7:24–30), failing to heal a blind man at his first touch (8:22–26), using parables to keep people from understanding his message (4:10–12), being so distressed in the Garden of Gethsemane (14:32–42), and crying out "My God, my God, why have you forsaken me?" when he dies (15:34). Ranging further, the lists include the disciples' failure to understand Jesus and the Gospel's disjointed style and abrupt ending—with the women running away from the tomb and saying nothing to anyone because they are afraid.[1]

This last moment in the Gospel of Mark leads me to the lists of what students are surprised not to find—resurrection and birth stories being the most obvious. Other elements of the story students expect to find in Mark but don't include the Lord's Prayer, any number of familiar parables and sayings, a more loving Jesus, a clear reason for why Jesus dies, and, occasionally, elements of the Passion Narrative—like the other "last words."

For students who know the Gospels well (and for many other readers also), the surprise at what Mark's version doesn't include is usually mild. After all, they know they can find the missing pieces in the other Gospels (or elsewhere). Their assumption is that each evangelist wrote what he had heard, so that to get the whole story requires reading all the Gospels and arranging them into one. Such an approach not only fills in the missing pieces, but also eases some of the difficult stories. This, of course, is a common way to think of the Gospels—and an ancient one.

Within a hundred years of the writing of the first Gospel (most probably the Gospel of Mark, around the year 70), a Syrian Christian named Tatian wove the four Gospels (and perhaps some other sources) into one continuous narrative, in effect creating

---

[1]The study bibles we use note the different endings in early manuscripts of the Gospel of Mark, with important manuscripts ending at 16:8.

one Gospel out of four—what the translator of an Arabic version of Tatian's harmony referred to as *The Earliest Life of Christ*.[2] Though others may have composed harmonies of the Gospels earlier, Tatian's was the most widely used, remaining the dominant text for Syriac Christians well into the sixth century. Two centuries after Tatian, Augustine wrote a treatise defending the harmonizing of the Gospels—as a way to combat charges that there were contradictions in the Gospels that undermine their integrity. A proper harmonization, Augustine argued, demonstrated that there were no contradictions in the Gospels, or at least none that significantly altered the essential truth of their story. Still, the long and complex process that led to the making of the Christian Bible as we know it stuck with the four Gospels and their notable differences.

Ever since, therefore, scholars (and others) who seek to recapture "what happened" usually begin with the various versions of individual stories and sayings in the four Gospels, first seeking to determine which of them is best and then arranging them into an order that somehow makes sense. Results vary, depending on how one determines the "best" version of a story or saying and what ordering of them "makes sense." Some variations in interpreting an individual story or saying depend on the methods readers use, but not all. Readers can use the very same methods (which scholars continue to hone) and still reach different conclusions. But this is hardly surprising. After all, there are four Gospels, which means there have been differences in telling the story from the very beginning. Nor are the differences simply matters of detail or wording.

---

[2] J. Hamlyn Hill, *The Earliest Life of Christ: The Diatessaron of Tatian* (Piscataway, NJ: Gorgias Press, 2001; this is a reprint of the second edition published by T & T Clark in 1910).

Consider, for example, the famous story of Jesus' walking on the water (Mt 14:22–33; Mk 6:45–52; Jn 6:16–21). Leaving aside for now the questions of how he could have done it, why Mark says he meant to pass by the struggling disciples, and why Matthew added Peter's attempt to join Jesus, what are we to make of the conclusion to the story? Mark writes that after Jesus gets into the boat and the wind ceases, the disciples are "utterly astounded, for they did not understand about the loaves, but their hearts were hardened." In Matthew's version, however, the disciples are neither "astounded" nor lacking in understanding. Rather, they "worshiped him, saying, 'Truly you are the Son of God.'" The conclusion to the story of the walking on the water in Matthew and Mark is radically different—whatever may have happened.[3] So different, the story becomes new in the telling.

For quite some time the consensus has been that the author of Matthew used the Gospel of Mark (or a version of it) in composing his own Gospel, reorganizing and reshaping Mark's stories to fit his purpose.[4] In the walking-on-the-water story, as in many others, Matthew's disciples come across better than Mark's: they recognize who Jesus is and respond accordingly. This allows Matthew to present the disciples as authorities for the future, the ones to whom Jesus will give the power to "bind and loose" (16:16, 18:18) and to make disciples of all nations (28:16–20). This does not mean, however, that Mark's version is a simple telling of the story as it happened. More and more, readers of Mark have come to see that its author also shapes individual stories in

---

[3] The ending of the story is different again in John's version: "and immediately the boat reached the land toward which they were going." Luke does not have the story.

[4] There is a lot more to Matthew's approach to writing a Gospel than this. But for the moment it is enough to note that Mark is one of the sources.

pursuit of a larger goal. In the walking-on-the-water story the disciples' fear is similar to the response many characters have in the Gospel of Mark (like the women at the tomb in 16:8). And their lack of understanding and hardness of heart show up again and again in Mark's stories of the disciples, so that Mark's version of this story fits the pattern perfectly. But why would Mark want to present the disciples as lacking in understanding? It is difficult to answer this question historically, but the buildup to Jesus' outburst in 8:14–21 suggests it is an important part of his storytelling. Jesus peppers the disciples with questions:

> "Do you still not perceive or understand? Are your hearts hardened? Do you have eyes, and fail to see? Do you have ears, and fail to hear? And do you not remember? When I broke the five loaves for the five thousand, how many baskets full of broken pieces did you collect?" They said to him, "Twelve." "And the seven for the four thousand, how many baskets full of broken pieces did you collect?" And they said to him, "Seven." Then he said to them, "Do you not yet understand?" (Mk 8:17–21)[5]

Jesus' frustration in this passage is palpable. And so it will be again when later in this chapter, after proclaiming Jesus to be the Messiah, Peter rebukes Jesus for saying that "the Son of Man must undergo great suffering, and be rejected by the elders, the chief priests, and the scribes, and be killed, and after three days rise again." Jesus, in turn, rebukes Peter with the withering comment, "Get behind me, Satan! For you are setting your mind not on divine things but on human things."

---

[5] In Matthew's version the disciples do understand (16:12), another instance in which a story is reshaped in support of the disciples.

Through the next two chapters, the central section of Mark's Gospel, Jesus will repeat this prediction of the Passion twice, and each time the disciples will not understand it (9:30–37; 10:32–45). The placement and patterning of these predictions strongly suggest that they belong to Mark's purpose in composing the Gospel. But there is a surprising element to them. Look again at the first prediction: Jesus says the Son of Man will suffer, be killed, and after three days rise again; Peter rebukes Jesus, apparently rejecting the notion that the Son of Man/Messiah could suffer and die.[6] What we would expect here is for Mark to have Jesus inform Peter *why* the Messiah must suffer, most likely using Jewish scripture to support his teaching. But he doesn't. Instead, Jesus "called the crowd with his disciples, and said to them, 'If any want to become my followers, let them deny themselves and take up their cross and follow me'" (8:34), going on to teach them about discipleship (8:35—9:1). The same pattern occurs in the other prediction sequences. Thus, Mark's concern here in the central section is not to demonstrate that the Messiah must suffer but to make clear what it means to be the disciple of a suffering Messiah. Consequently, Mark uses the misunderstanding of the disciples to engage his readers. If they, like the disciples, seek places of honor in the coming kingdom (as James and John do in the last instance of the pattern) and get angry with one another in disputes about status, they misunderstand the meaning of discipleship (10:35–45).

I have taken time with these few examples to show how Matthew and Mark tell their stories, to show that they were writers who exercised considerable freedom and creativity in reshaping

---

[6] Mark appears to link the two terms, which otherwise are distinct.

and organizing their material. The same can be said of Luke and John.

Luke is quite open about his purpose and method in writing. In the preface to his Gospel, after noting that many others had "undertaken to set down an orderly account of the events that have been fulfilled among us, just as they were handed on to us by those who from the beginning were eyewitnesses and servants of the word," he goes on to say, "I too decided, after investigating everything carefully from the very first, to write an orderly account for you, most excellent Theophilus, so that you may know the truth concerning the things about which you have been instructed" (Lk 1:1–4). It is clear in Luke's selection, adaptation, and organization of material in his Gospel (and later in a second volume called The Acts of the Apostles), that his notion of truth was not limited to accuracy in recording what happened. He too interprets the story, consciously working as a writer.[7]

The author of the Gospel of John has long been regarded as a writer who went beyond the reporting of what happened, his work being referred to as "the spiritual Gospel" already in the second century.[8] One sees this in his overtly theological themes, rich metaphorical language, numerous interpretive asides, and most prominently, statements such as "Now Jesus did many other signs in the presence of his disciples, which are not written in this book. But these are written so that you may come to believe that Jesus is the Messiah, the Son of God, and that through believing you may have life in his name" (20:30–31).

---

[7] The opening verses of Luke and Acts intentionally echo similar prefaces in the works of Hellenistic historians, including those of Jewish writers like Josephus.

[8] See the comment in Eusebius, *Ecclesiastical History* 6.14.5–7.

Matthew, Mark, and Luke are not as overt as John. But as Mark's short aside, "Let the reader understand,"[9] demonstrates, he too is consciously a writer and has expectations of his readers. It is clear that the other evangelists have the same awareness and the same expectations. Each has told a story, and with each telling it becomes new. This is true even of the Passion Narrative.

In all four Gospels, the story of the Passion, the last week of Jesus' life, is the most extended narrative: Matthew 21–27; Mark 11–16; Luke 19:28–23:56; John 12–19.[10] Thus, Martin Kähler's description of Mark as "a Passion Narrative with an extended introduction" can also be applied to the other canonical Gospels as well. This is not to say, I must emphasize strongly, that all four Gospels treat the Passion equally or have the same understanding of it. The differences between and among them are too significant to gloss over. But in the ways they foreshadow the Passion[11] and by the careful attention they give to their narrating of the story, the evangelists demonstrate that they cannot conceive of Jesus' life without recounting the story of his death.[12] The challenge

---

[9] Four words in English, three in Greek.

[10] I consider John 12:1–8 the beginning of John's Passion Narrative, since it contains the story of the anointing of Jesus and leads to this Gospel's account of "the triumphal entry" into Jerusalem and what counts as its "last supper."

[11] The Passion predictions in Mark, Matthew, and less prominently in Luke are only one way the writers of these Gospels point to the death of Jesus in the earlier parts of their narratives. In the Gospel of John, Jesus' death is foreshadowed in John the Baptist's famous words, "Here is the Lamb of God who takes away the sin of the world!" in the first chapter (v. 29).

[12] For many, it may seem obvious that the story of Jesus' death would be an essential part of the story. But the Gospel of Thomas and the collection of sayings commonly called Q demonstrate that some early Christians could express their reverence for Jesus without reference to his death, focusing instead on his teaching.

for us as readers is to attend to their distinct voices even as we blend them into one.

Since the evangelists are writers, other writers can be helpful guides for us readers. They don't replace what scholars do with the text, but they can help us see it in new ways. The essays that follow do just that.

1

Matthew's Gospel

Galilean Tenderness Under a Warming Sky

John Elder

In Memory of My Parents

Tugging at the Knot

The last five chapters of Matthew's Gospel form a knot I can't untie.

Upon being asked to respond to Matthew within this collection of personal essays on the Passion Narratives, I soon came to realize that I had always veered away from certain disturbing aspects of this Gospel. Although ours was a Bible-reading family, we didn't bear down, as scholars would, on one whole book at a time. We either returned again and again to certain inspiring passages or, conversely, contemplated the broad sweep of history, prophecy, and poetry to which individual books contributed. This meant that, as a child, I experienced the Synoptic Gospels as filling out a shared story in complementary ways, rather than

as challenging each other with their own distinctive and charac-
teristic versions. Focusing now on Matthew's Passion Narrative,
I am thus confronted by disturbing elements I was not forced to
grapple with in our family's readings around the kitchen table.

Early in life I took the story of Jesus to heart. I remember
clearly how downcast his abandonment by his closest friends
made me feel as a child. Even after Jesus says to Peter and the
other disciples, "So, could you not stay awake with me one hour?"
(26:40), he returns twice from anguished prayer to find they have
all fallen asleep again. In 26:45, right before his arrest, he resigns
himself to this state of affairs, saying, "Are you still sleeping and
taking your rest? See, the hour is at hand, and the Son of Man is
betrayed into the hands of sinners." It is evident as I read it this
morning that Matthew's extraordinarily dramatic account of the
Passion gains much of its power from the prolonged, excruciat-
ing story of loneliness that both anticipates and defers the public
agony of crucifixion: the ache precedes the wound. The isolation
Jesus feels in the garden after his disciples have drifted away from
him into sleep distresses him more than the torch-lit arrival of
"a large crowd with swords and clubs, from the chief priests and
the elders of the people" (v. 47) led to him by Judas.

From that moment and on through his responses to Pilate and
his other questioners, Jesus holds himself strikingly remote from
the whirl of false testimony, cross-examination, hypocrisy, self-
justification, and condemnation. In 27:11 he responds to Pilate's
question only with "You say so." Verse 12 has him foregoing any
answer to accusations by the chief priests and elders, and in verse
14, when Pilate asks if he has heard what they had said about him,
Jesus "did not answer." In Matthew (and even more clearly in the
Gospel of John) his attention is already focused inward, on the

coming, galvanic events, which he alone fully foresees and understands. When the cock crows at dawn and Peter realizes that he has betrayed his master three times since Gethsemane, just as prophesied, my sympathy for this disciple's failure of steadiness always made me feel implicated in his shame. These are, of course, an adult's words for a boy's experience. They intellectualize, and in that way falsify, my earlier confusion—caught up in a story that was at once beyond my comprehension and inescapable. Now, if in a different way, I'm entangled in it still.

My current reading of Matthew's Passion Narrative, well over half a century after my first introduction to it, registers other distressing aspects of the narrative as well as the ones that struck me earlier. So much of modern history, including the jumbled details of the morning's online news, reverberates with that old account of cruelty and dread. The Good Shepherd, the kindly teacher and healer, is caught up in the remorseless gears of political and military authority. An armed tribunal takes him prisoner and passes sentence upon him. Righteous and triumphant torturers take over from there.

Matthew's personal rage at Christ's humiliation and execution introduces yet another harrowing element into his passion for me, now. The writer's mortification at being ostracized by his own Jewish community because of his belief in Jesus as the Messiah instills a rancorous quality into his depiction of the priests and Pharisees that is far more vitriolic than anything found in the other Gospels. The consequences of such fury become most disastrous in the narrative when Pilate, convinced that Jesus is innocent of the claims of sacrilege lodged against him, offers to release him to the people. Incited by the priests and Pharisees, though, the crowd calls for the release of the murderer Barabbas instead. As for Jesus, they cry out, "Let him be crucified" (27:23). And they insist in 27:25, "His blood be on us, and on our children." These lines have been seized upon by anti-Semites over the centuries and have without a doubt encouraged pogroms as well as the Holocaust itself.

Recent years have brought serious attempts by Christian leaders to address this deep stain in the fabric of our tradition. But reconciliation is hard to find within the knotted fury of Matthew's Passion. Speaking for myself, I possess neither the steady faith nor the keen theological insight that might allow me to slice through this conundrum. All I can do is carry the knot, in my stomach, as a sort of koan. I am involved in this Passion through a love of Jesus that is inseparable from the early guidance of my parents, which I retain even after turning away from the stern certainties that many have derived from texts like Matthew 25—28.

Matthew 25, alone among the Gospels, frames the Passion with a vivid picture of the Last Judgment. Humanity will ultimately be divided into the sheep and the goats, with the former gathered into heavenly joy and the latter condemned to everlasting pain. Chapter 28, after the intervening account of Jesus' suffering, death, and resurrection, depicts a transfigured Lord, who delivers his Great Commission to evangelize the whole world as a prologue to such winnowing of the saved from the damned. The Passion itself thus represents a crucible in which Jesus of Nazareth is turned into the Christ, in which the condemned sufferer becomes the supreme magistrate. Overwhelming power remains the central truth, though its locus shifts. Alfred North Whitehead wrote in *Process and Reality* that when the Roman Empire adopted Christianity as the state religion, "Caesar conquered; and the received text of Western theology was edited by his lawyers." Matthew's Passion contributed to this process of imperial appropriation.

My lifelong vocation has been as a teacher of literature, and the power of vivid scenes has always trumped more systematic or theoretical approaches to reading for me. One scene from fiction and one indelible experience in my own life are especially helpful to me now as models for the way in which loving scenes may live on beyond their stories' daunting conclusions. Both reveal that sometimes the last word can come in the middle of a tale. The first scene I'm thinking of comes in one of the most violent and chaotic chapters of *Moby-Dick*, "The Grand Armada." A boat is launched from the *Pequod* to pursue a congregation of migrating sperm whales. After Queequeg manages to harpoon one whale, Ishmael and the rest of the crew are pulled wildly through the sea by the stricken creature. When the whale finally dives and dislodges the harpoon, they veer suddenly into a calm circle amid the tumult of flight and pursuit, "as if from some mountain torrents we had slid into a serene valley lake."

Looking down, they could see mother whales gliding around their nursing calves, "the women and children of this routed host." The young whales came up to rub the gunwales, while "Queequeg patted their foreheads" and "Starbuck scratched their backs with his lance."

> And thus, though surrounded by circle upon circle of consternations and affrights, did these inscrutable creatures at the centre freely and fearlessly indulge in all peaceful concernments; yea, serenely reveled in dalliance and delight. But even so, amid the tornadoed Atlantic of my being, do

I myself still for ever centrally disport in mute calm; and while ponderous planets of unwaning woe revolve round me, deep down and deep inland there I still bathe me in eternal mildness of joy.

Ishmael's capacity to resist the fury of Captain Ahab, who is so fiercely determined to separate white from black, righteousness from evil, is reinforced by this vision of nurturing communion. In the quiet interior of the sea something is glimpsed that lies below and beyond the harpooned and exhausted whales spouting blood, the blubber distilled into kegs of wealth, and the scraps from the try-works thrown overboard to roiling sharks. When Ishmael finally floats alone in the sea, after the great ship has gone down, he does so without fear; remembering the vision of a world beyond conflict, he is borne up in faith that he will find a way to tell his story. In trying to engage with Matthew's Passion while at the same time holding out against its punitive and judgmental tone, I too am buoyed up by remembering the nurturing, beautiful home life in which my parents enacted their own deep Christian faith.

Affirmation can arise in the midst of a story whose ending might seem to allow no possibilities other than apocalypse or nihilism. My most direct experience of this truth derives from my father's final illness. He was an exemplary man, serene and kindly, deeply read but never dogmatic, a devout Christian with no sense of narrow sectarianism but with a strong, sympathetic interest both in other religions and in science, a man whose days were filled with mirth and music. Dad's favorite word in the Greek New Testament was *agapé*—a tender concern for others.

And then he developed Alzheimer's. Shortly before his death, when the family assembled at the nursing home for his seventy-sixth birthday, we wheeled him into a room with a cake on the table and balloons hanging from strings taped to the acoustical tile on the ceiling. But when we began to sing "Happy Birthday," his face crumpled in fear. He didn't know where he was or what we were doing. Perhaps even who we were. Realizing that we had made a grievous mistake, we all quickly stopped singing and helped him back to his quiet room, where he would have less reason to be alarmed.

We may have fallen into this error because of our inability to believe Dad could ever lose the resilient, nonassertive pleasure in life that had made him seem to me like the *I Ching*'s "superior man," the one who flows like water rather than contending for eminence. He *had* lived such a life of flow, from an impoverished boyhood on through horrible experiences in World War II. His heart had never succumbed to strife, and his impulse was always to encourage others in their own quests for balance and peace. In the midst of his religious vocation, and of the family life in which my mother and he gently fostered my older brother, Lyn, and me, he sought moments of connection in which the ponderous circumstances of life might be lifted up. One of the last sentences I heard him utter as I was sitting by his bedside, just before he lost the power to speak, was "Things change." Even after that, though, he would join in the hymns sung by members of Tiburon Baptist Church who came to visit. His strong baritone was husky now, but he knew all the verses and still liked to switch back and forth between the bass and tenor harmonies.

My father was a Southern Baptist minister and seminary pro-fessor who also loved the philosophy of Whitehead. It excited him because of its bold attempt to reconcile faith and science into a non-monolithic but unified and dynamic system. While I was at college, Dad sent me copies of Whitehead's *Process and Reality* and *Science and the Modern World*, as well as John Cobb's *Process Theology*. In returning to the heat of the Passion now, while also trying to affirm the loving center of my own biblical experience, rather than reside at an apocalyptic edge, I take courage from a late chapter in *Process and Reality* called "God and the World." After having discussed the dominant visions of the divine order modeled on the power of the divine Caesars, the moral absolutes of the Hebrew prophets, and the logical hierarchies of Aristotle, Whitehead writes:

> There is, however, in the Galilean origin of Christianity yet another suggestion which does not fit very well with any of the three main strands of thought. It does not emphasize the ruling Caesar, or the ruthless moralist, or the unmoved mover. It dwells upon the tender elements in the world, which slowly and in quietness operate by love; and it finds purpose in the present immediacy of a kingdom not of this world. Love neither rules, nor is it unmoved; also it is a little oblivious as to morals. It does not look to the future; for it finds its own reward in the immediate present.

Several pages later Whitehead elaborates further on this vision:

> The image—and it is but an image—the image under which this operative growth of God's nature is best conceived, is that of a tender care that nothing be lost. . . . It is the judgment of a tenderness which loses nothing that can be saved. It is also the judgment of a wisdom which uses what in the temporal world is mere wreckage.

While such gentleness is not evident within the heat of Matthew's Passion, it is essential to the larger career of Jesus. As captured in the image of a tiny seed growing into a mighty tree, or of leaven folded into the dough for bread that will feed a family, his life was a ministry of hope, not admonishment. While reading chapters 25 through 28 of this Gospel, it is important not to forget 5:44–45: "But I say to you, Love your enemies and pray for those who persecute you, so that you may be children of your Father in heaven; for he makes his sun rise on the evil and on the good, and sends rain on the righteous and on the unrighteous."

The instances of "tender care" that Whitehead contrasts to "the kingdom . . . of this world" are not by that token separate from history. Rather, it is because they are so vital, modest, central, and immediate that they can escape notice by an eye obsessed with ideology and power. Nonetheless, in offering the possibility of "a judgment of a tenderness" they help to heal a world rent by the furious judgments of division and vindication. They bring redemption to a world of wreckage. Just as moments of grace can live on in the heart amid climactic violence and loss, so, too, does a promise of tenderness endure within the DNA of Christianity. This remains true today, even after decades in which judgmentalism and self-righteousness have loudly claimed the tradition as their own. If the potential of Galilean tenderness is now to be more fully realized, however, it must be through vigorous engagement with the ecological and political challenges of our day. It must reclaim a suitable, non-punitive expression of its own passionate intensity. Such a hope also requires me, on a personal level, to explore my own history as a reader of the Bible. I need to understand how my current environmentalist values are rooted in early religious experiences if I am to respond more constructively to the ecological crisis of our time.

Beginning at the Kitchen Table

Our family read the Bible every day. We studied passages from the Old and New Testaments for Sunday School and Training Union, the classes coordinated with morning and evening services on the Sabbath. These selections were designed to take us through the entire Bible over a several-year cycle. On Wednesday evenings we gathered with a smaller group from the congregation for Prayer Meeting. This midweek service was less formal, with lots of hymn singing in the four-part harmony that is the glory of Southern Baptist worship. There was Bible reading and prayer in that setting, too, though with passages chosen more spontaneously than in the Sunday curriculum. The context for all these services and classes was our nightly experience of reading the scriptures together, as my mother and father, my older brother, Lyn, and I gathered around the kitchen table for supper. These were my favorite exposures to the Bible, both because of the pleasure I felt in reading and conversation with my parents and because we generally focused on the stories and poetry rather than on the historical and theological content of Sunday's more systematic study.

Just as we didn't spend much time around the family table on Pauline Christology, we rarely dwelled on the priestly prohibitions and apocalyptic fantasias so exciting to the wowsers of today's so-called Religious Right. What the four of us loved were the dramas of Genesis and Exodus, Joshua, First and Second Kings, Jonah, and Ruth, the poetry of the Psalms and Job, and the Gospels. I can still remember how flavorful these books felt to me as a ten year old. The shadowed grandeur of Moses and David and the eloquence of Job were so much more bracing than the tepid fare we generally read in school. When our readings turned to the Gospels, we lingered over events like Jesus' healing of the crippled and the blind. We also focused on the parables, where I caught my first intoxicating glimpse of a landscape where spiritual truth and natural fact may embrace. By the time I entered junior high, our family's Bible study had stopped, in part because my brother's teenage activities made it harder to schedule regular sessions together around the kitchen table. But my path was already set. My love of literature and my vocation as a teacher and writer grew directly from the experience of reading the majestic language of the King James translation aloud in our family.

I wonder whether the positive and inviting tone of our early Bible reading may have been set especially by my mother, whose sweet nature seems to have borne her along equally from girlhood on a red-dirt farm in northern Louisiana to her meeting with my father in the Baptist Student Union at LSU to her return to the farm as she waited out his service as a paratrooper during World War II and finally to my parents' move to California when he started teaching at a Baptist seminary there. Though she didn't read the scriptures in Greek and Hebrew as my father did, she studied the Bible assiduously throughout her life.

Dad, Lyn, and I all owned beautiful copies of the Bible, printed by Cambridge University Press on India paper and bound in black Morocco leather. My two most glamorous possessions as a boy were this stately volume and my supple Richie Ashburn–model fielder's mitt. Mom had a lovely leather binding on her bible, too, but chose to order it in her favorite color of sky blue. I've never seen another bible of just that color. Its strongest associations for me (beyond the fact that it matched both my mother's eyes and the woodwork in our Mill Valley kitchen) are with the tender blues and greens of a vernal landscape photograph that hung on the wall beside my bed when I was a child. Super-imposed on this image were the kindly countenance of Jesus and the text of Psalm 23.

This psalm was the first poem I ever memorized, learning it line by line from my mother before I could read. The comforting cadences of the shepherd David, like the goodness and mercy of my parents, have followed me all the days of my life. Just as, from the time of Plato, lovers of music have identified certain intervals and keys with particular colors, the language of Psalm 23 remains inseparable for me from the green of its pastures and the blue of its still waters. Another personal association with this poem is with my mother's cool hand (fragrant with the almond scent of Jergens Lotion), resting on my forehead as she tried to help one young dervish stop spinning at the end of the day.

My mother's hand also figures in my memory of a memorable revival we attended in Bastrop, Louisiana, one summer when I was a boy. The billowing beige tent was set up across Mer Rouge Road from the dairy farm where my mother had grown up, on a field donated for that purpose by my beloved namesake Uncle John. The service opened with a few announcements and jokes, then moved straight into the hymn singing. We began serenely with hymns of faith:

> Jesus is the friend you need
> (the friend you need),
> such a friend is He indeed
> (is He indeed).

Over the course of the next half hour the key modulated to longing. We sang "Tell Me the Old, Old Story" and "Softly and Tenderly," with its organ-tone refrain "Come home (come home),

Come home (come home), Ye who are weary come home." Then it was time for the sermon.

Our redheaded traveling revivalist's approach contrasted starkly to the witty, reflective preaching I was used to hearing from my father at our family's church in New Orleans. With little by way of prologue the revivalist was shouting, haranguing, and, yes, pounding the pulpit. I had never heard, or imagined, a voice of such fury and passion. All of us gathered in that gusty canvas enclosure had been condemned to hellfire by a just God. Yet we were, amazingly, offered salvation if we could open ourselves up to the present moment of grace through our wholehearted repentance. This masterful sermon had one keenly honed intent—getting members of the congregation to stumble forward at the altar call. As the revivalist exhorted listeners with his emotion-saturated voice, and as we all sang "Just as I am," over and over and over again, a current of those who wanted to rededicate their lives pulsed up the central aisle. Twenty, thirty, fifty people from the several hundred in that congregation walked up to receive the minister's hand of blessing on their heads. After doing so, they sat dazed and sobbing in a pew at the front, where they would be embraced by their friends and family after the service ended. I can still remember how oppressive this sustained and mysterious intensity felt to me as a child.

Such a spectacle of unmediated adult emotion was hard to make sense of. I felt frightened by the anguish and jubilation voiced by people in the surrounding benches. I was also troubled, as I have remained ever since, by a conflict between the image of a loving God and his gentle Son Jesus and the sentence of eternal suffering for all who were not reprieved by grace. It wasn't that I imagined that everyone around me was perfect.

But the main thing my parents had shown me every day of my life was kindness and encouragement, and I couldn't imagine a more generous uncle than the one who sat on the other side of me. I was aware of various sneaky stratagems through which I sometimes managed to get my own way, but none of them felt like hanging crimes. Even my older brother, Lyn, who liked to knuckle me hard in the upper arm when Mom wasn't looking, didn't seem to deserve eternal fire—though I thought he might well be improved by a couple of solid parental whacks.

The revivalist kept pleading with us. He seemed to be on the verge of weeping himself now but knew that there were still people in the congregation who could hear Jesus calling them. Several more would go up, then there would be another long, painful delay as the music swelled and the preacher shouted. I began to wonder whether if *I* went up that might finally allow the evening to end. But then I could feel my mother's cool hand on my arm. Not exactly holding on. She was simply reassuring me that I was fine beside her, just as I was.

Over the intervening years I've continued to ponder this seeming disconnect between the harshness and the gentleness within my religious heritage. I have never been able to believe in the stark tale of damnation versus redemption that many find essential to Christian faith. Nor do I now ascribe a unique or exclusive value to Protestant Christianity among the world's spiritual traditions. From my wife, Rita's, Catholic practice and from my personal contacts with Judaism, Buddhism, and Native American beliefs, I have received inspiration both akin to and complementary to the best of my Southern Baptist training. Like many Americans I know that I must also find a way to glimpse the heart of Islam now, and the way in which it sustains all those millions of the faithful whose lives never register in our explosive headlines. But in the midst of all these valuable influences I continue to pray as I was taught and to love Jesus. In trying to sort this all out, and to help activate the constructive power of my own tradition in a time marred by consumerism, violence, and environmental damage, I've turned back to the Bible as a resource. What I've found there has been the same conflict that I felt in that long-ago revival. In compressed form, my struggle is somehow to reconcile the spiritually charged and flowering world of the psalms and parables with the apocalyptic heat of Matthew's Passion.

By 1961, as I entered Tamalpais Union High School in Mill Valley, California, I had begun to identify passionately with the wilderness movement. It seems clear in retrospect that this new sense of affiliation grew pretty directly from my early exposure to the psalms and parables, with their celebration of earth's sacred fund of truth. A couple of years later my friends and I got our driver's licenses and began to take excursions to the high Sierra, Yosemite Valley, and Tuolomne Meadows. Such landscapes, much as our family's Bible reading had done, loomed over and enhanced both my personal relationships and my private reflections. The gorgeous, large-format Sierra Club books in the Mill Valley Library reinforced this sense of a parallel. Ansel Adams's sublime monochrome prints of Yosemite were awesome in ways that reverberated with Genesis and Job, while Eliot Porter's images of trees, wildflowers, and lichen-speckled boulders were reminiscent of Jesus' parables of the kingdom. The tender blues and greens of Richard Kaufmann's photographs, in a Sierra Club edition of John Muir's writings entitled *Gentle Wilderness*, felt strikingly close to the palette of the Twenty-third Psalm.

Like other children I both grew into and away from my family with the passing years. Just as reading the Bible had pointed me

toward the Sierra, it encouraged me to become a devout reader
of other books, too. One of my reasons for choosing to attend
Pomona College was to stay on the West Coast and be able to
hitchhike up to Mill Valley from Claremont every month or so
and see my parents. Another was the excellent reputation of its
faculty in philosophy, the field in which I thought I wanted to
major. Though I could sense the intellectual power of Leibniz,
Locke, and Hobbes, however, my freshman-year class on modern
philosophy felt like pretty arid terrain. If there was poetry or
drama in those cheaply printed little paperbacks, I was unable
to find them. Studying sonnets in an introductory course on
poetry with Darcy O'Brien opened up the possibility of a more
embodied mode of reading. I became an English major so that I
could get my college degree while reading books that astonished
and delighted me, and whose language had a meaning beyond
the denotative. I noted with interest that quite a few of my fellow students of English had their own strong backgrounds in
various traditions of the Book; for them, as for me, vast meanings swam through and around these vital new voices. Like that
Sunday School boy D. H. Lawrence, we turned to literature as
the "Bright Book of Life."

When I decided, after Pomona, to attend graduate school at
Yale, my experience of literary study became a more complicated
one. The most valuable part of it was the regimen of reading
from early in the morning to late at night. In a single, nourishing
class with David Thorburn we read practically all the novels of
Eliot, Hardy, Conrad, and Woolf. In other seminars we read the
collected works of Chaucer, Shakespeare, Whitman, Dickens, and
Frost. Bart Giamatti's course on Spenser rooted our reading of
The Fairie Queen in the enchanting worlds of Ariosto and Tasso. I
can vividly remember the class in which he related the anxiety

at the heart of Renaissance humanism to the Italian words *fre-nare* and *sfrenare*. The first expressed a determination to rein in and control our impulses, the second an ever-present possibility of losing control and galloping toward social and individual destruction. Submerging in such seas of imagination and poetry was intoxicating.

I was less attracted by certain professionalistic and technical aspects of literary criticism at this level. I arrived at Yale in 1969, soon after the champions of high theory had seized the ramparts. In the course of one panel discussion at the graduate school a tenured enthusiast proclaimed that he would as soon read the Manhattan telephone directory as *Bleak House*; in each case there was an intricate system of language available to decipher and deconstruct. But just as I had held an inward reservation about hellfire as a child in Louisiana, so too I resisted the incineration of compelling plots and characters as a grad student in the suave pastures of Connecticut.

The requirements for coursework were not extensive: just three semesters of classes before beginning to formulate a thesis. When I discovered that it was possible to include courses outside of English in fulfilling this requirement, I signed up for one on New Testament theology taught at the Divinity School by an amiable Dutch professor named Frederik Wisse. This was where I discovered the New Hermeneutics, an unanticipated bridge between the New Critical close readings, which were prevalent in my college courses and current theoretical approaches down the hill at the Hall of Graduate Studies. I was also fascinated by a volume we read called *Gospel Parallels*, in which the Synoptic Gospels were arrayed side by side in columns that showed where the narratives intertwined or diverged. The Gospels of Matthew and Luke elaborated on Mark's earlier version in ways that brought out the writers' differing attitudes toward both Christianity's Jewish heritage and the divinity of Jesus. Matthew's parables of the kingdom were of special interest to me, and I enjoyed reading scholars like C. H. Dodd, who delved as deeply into them as one would into a sonnet by Shakespeare or Wordsworth.

That course with Professor Wisse turned out to be the total of my formal training in biblical studies. Nor have I ended up building my life around a church, as my parents did. The Quakers, with their steady witness against the Vietnam War, were an inspiring community for me to encounter during graduate school and again at the beginning of my career at Middlebury College. Following that chapter, a vital new Zen Center in Shelburne, Vermont, was also of great value to me, with its training based on koans that were strikingly reminiscent of certain parables of Jesus. As familial and professional challenges continued to ratchet up, though, weekend outings into the Green Mountains refreshed me more than anything else as I tried to prepare myself for the coming week. Each season—from the yellow of early foliage season to its russet aftermath, from blue-shadowed snow on midwinter afternoons to the Dutchman's breeches and trillium of early spring, and on to July, with splashing forays along the pools and boulders of the New Haven River—offered its own collection of parables. Occasionally, too, I would drive down to Woodstock for services at Weston Priory with Rita, whose Catholic faith is as steadfast as my parents' Baptist belief was. The chance to read the Bible and sing hymns in that congregation felt nourishing and also harmonious with the simplicity of its monastic community and the grandeur of the surrounding woods. Though theologically diffuse and without the solid sense of a religious community I would have hoped for, I could nevertheless still identify with Wendell Berry's self-description as "a forest Christian."

A couple of years ago I was challenged to look harder for a shape within this personal jumble of experiences and affinities. Bill McKibben asked me to help out with planning an environmentally oriented worship service in the Methodist Church of Ripton, Vermont, where he lives with his wife, Sue Halpern, and their daughter, Sophie. This white clapboard structure just up Route 125 from the general store used to enlist Rabbi Victor Reichert as its seasonal minister. Rabbi Reichert and his wife, Louise, traveled to Ripton every summer from their home in Cincinnati, where he taught in a seminary associated with the Conservative branch of American Judaism. Robert Frost and he became close friends, and the two of them frequently enjoyed discussing the Bible together. The local Methodists had relished the annual adventure of having a rabbi as their pastor. So this beautiful little church felt like an especially promising place for an experiment into whether the scriptures, which Jewish and Christian traditions claim as holy ground, could be reclaimed as a resource by activists concerned about climate change and the disruption of natural systems. Prayer and the Bible, like the American flag, were too powerful simply to cede to George W. Bush's sanctimonious and anti-environmental supporters.

Several dozen people gathered in the Ripton Meeting House on an overcast but pleasant summer evening. To the accompaniment of the wheezy old pump-organ we began by singing a few hymns like "For the Beauty of the Earth." After I read Psalm 100, "The heavens declare the glory of God," along with an evocation of the earth's sublime wildness from the Book of Job, Rita's and my son Caleb played an improvised meditation on the viola.

Then Bill offered a compact, provocative sermon based on Job's celebration of wilderness in chapters 38 through 40. He paused over sublime lines like God's challenge to Job's know-it-all "comforters"—"Where were you when I laid the foundations of the earth?"—and he dwelled especially on the loving evocation of undomesticated animals, with no discernible use to humans, for whom God had nevertheless created wildness as a "house," and "barren lands" as their "dwellings." Such descriptions, Bill suggested, should chasten our sense of human prerogatives. After a couple more hymns and a prayer the service concluded with a chance for members of our little impromptu congregation to chat about what we had just experienced together. Several comments mirrored my own feelings of both pleasure and relief in beginning to draw together our environmental ethic with our religious backgrounds.

But one remark, offered near the end of that gathering by a lifelong member of that Methodist Church, also struck a troubling chord in my heart. With a friendly smile this gentleman rose from the venerable pew where he'd been sitting—with its white-painted back and seat and its brown, varnished arms. He wanted to remind us all to proclaim that Jesus Christ is Lord. This summed up my conundrum. To what extent is it possible for an individual like myself to claim the religious heritage and language of Christianity if not also declaring its unique value? Could there be validity in an approach that valued some aspects of Christian practice and belief while also appreciating the spiritual insights of Buddhism, for instance? I remembered sitting beside an American Jesuit, posted to the Vatican, during dinner at a UN-sponsored conference on environmental stewardship. He assured me that such a "smorgasbord" approach to religion was simply a manifestation of New Age longings for spirituality without rigor or responsibility. In resisting such claims for the exclusive validity of traditional systems of belief and practice, though, I feel obliged to attempt a more forceful connection between those aspects of the biblical tradition with special value for me and the daunting ecological and ethical issues of our time. I am strengthened in this impulse by Karen Armstrong's statement, in *The Bible: A Biography*, that "Midrash and exegesis were always supposed to relate directly to the burning issues of the day, and the fundamentalists should not be the only people who attempt this."

Facing the Heat

One reason, beyond its connection with my parents' faith, that I find myself knotted up in Matthew's Passion now is its association with the nature-based spirituality that emerged from and expresses my Christian background. The parables in that Gospel tilted gradually toward apocalypse and judgment. But so too has my love of the verdant beauty around my boyhood home in California and our own family's Vermont home been increasingly shadowed by the global crises of our day. David Brower, arguably the most influential conservationist of the twentieth century, used to deliver a speech he called "The Sermon." In it he detailed the destruction already visited upon wild beauty and natural systems by toxic chemicals, nuclear waste, industrial and transportation systems based on fossil fuels, and an exploding human population. And he evoked the prospect of a much more drastic ecological collapse if we in the West do not mend our ways. Dave Foreman, a founder of Earth First! and subsequently of the Wildlands Project, was, like Brower (and like me), a product of a fundamentalist home. He steadily carried on this oratory of peril, with its altar call for national and personal conversion. It's appropriate, then, for environmentalists to recognize the Calvinist heritage within such rhetoric, and the direct line that stretches back from it to the last four chapters of Matthew.

On the one hand, such a link should make us more careful about our own tendencies toward judgmentalism and righteousness—a division of the environmental sheep from the goats, and an impulse to order SUV drivers to climb out of their vehicles with their hands where we can see them. On the other, it reveals a powerful element of Matthew's Passion that I might have been in danger of missing for temperamental reasons: the inseparability of the nurturing loveliness of nature and our intimate relationships from the recurrence of fiery moments of decision. If the importance of either mode is unrecognized, both the web of life and our bonds to one another may be endangered. It has always been easier for me to perceive the danger to tenderness and empathy within the furor of judgment. Equally important, though, is the ability to stand up at moments of decision and engage in the larger struggles of our world. From Jonathan Edwards's painstaking attempts to awaken his congregation to their peril in ways that were visceral, not simply intellectual, to Brower's sermon, the passionate call for judgment and choice is an attempt to catalyze diffuse energies, to brush up the current from which a spark might leap. Today, facing an ecological crisis that is reflective of a profoundly isolated and selfish aspect of our culture, we need to acknowledge the error of our ways and take a new direction.

The sermons that speak most powerfully to me now have to do with climate change. They come from people like James Hansen, chief climate scientist at NASA, and Bill McKibben. Both of them call attention to the fact that, while global warming and climate destabilization are inevitable, the changes will shift from a serious scale to an utterly cataclysmic one if we can't soon bring the proportion of carbon in the atmosphere back down below 350 parts per million. The facts are so sobering as to require little polemic or metaphorical amplification: the melting of the Arctic ice, a rise of the oceans that endangers impoverished coastal communities around the world, an increase in the frequency and severity of hurricanes, and the desertification of continental interiors. Unless we can turn away from practices that continue to pour carbon into the sky we will turn our still waters and green pastures into a parched and inhospitable wasteland. If we don't change our lives there will be hell to pay. Since the present concentration of carbon in the atmosphere already hovers around 387 parts per million, this will require us to make immediate and significant changes to our personal and collective practices. Both conservation and the development of renewable sources of energy will be important parts of this change. But, most fundamental, it will require a willingness to restrain our appetites.

Ecologists use the term *ecotone* to describe the biologically rich habitats that contain species from each constituent habitat as well as species unique to that zone. *Edge effect*, in this scientific vocabulary, describes a proliferation of biotic energy and mass that arises within such dynamic, precarious, ambiguous environments. The richness of my own religious experience has been enhanced by the encounter between my Southern Baptist upbringing and the Zen Buddhist influences of my high school and college years in California, just as my religious heritage has become fruitfully entangled with the environmentalist movement's values. But there are also edges within edges. My sense of an affinity between the parables of the kingdom and the sacred beauty of Yosemite Valley torques into a dynamic tension with the sternness of the Last Judgment and the furor of the Passion, on the one hand, and with the urgent dangers of climate change, on the other.

I think about this edge while walking the cool slopes of our Vermont sugarbush with our dog Shadow, tightening saplines and tapping trees in preparation for the new sugaring season. This is a green and beautiful world in spring and summer, when I do such work. It is also the scene of shared projects that bind Rita and me together with our grown children and their own families, and connect us with the cycle of the year in our home landscape. But the combination of a gradual warming trend and a blurring of the transitions between seasons has already damaged the regeneration of our maple forests. The disruption of our familiar patterns alarms and disturbs me, as the torch-lit cruelty of the Passion did when I was a boy reading the Bible. Just as the Gospel writer turned to natural images like sheep and goats, wheat and tares to convey spiritual truths, so too, in the destabilization of the earth's climate we can discover a sharply focused image of today's drastic cultural crisis. The painfulness of the crucifixion is much more intense for a reader in love with Jesus, a love nourished by the beautifully natural context of his parables and other teachings. Dread of climate change and the impulse to work for new practices at the levels of policy, community, and family life are both more intense because of the love we bear for particular landscapes and the concern we feel for coming generations. Because of love there comes a time when we must turn to face the heat. But my own ethical center is neither in the Passion nor in the world of activism; it is in the zone *between* those fiery realities and my own daily, local experience of loving affiliation.

Unlike me, my parents remained devout Southern Baptists to the end of their lives. But as I return again in memory to their lives, I can glimpse the edge at which they found their own energetic sense of purpose. Much of the joy they found in their church, as members of the Southern diaspora to California in the mid-twentieth century, came from the experience of old-fashioned fellowship in a new setting that was at once exhilarating and intimidating. Frequent after-worship socials on the church grounds featured the fried chicken, fresh rolls, potato salad, three-bean salad, lemonade, and ice cream that were their childhood's taste of Sunday. I can remember the adults strolling amid picnic cloths spread on the grass, greeting each other as "Brother" and "Sister." There was always a joke to share and laughter was in the air. We had moved to California from Louisiana when I was eight, and I also remember noticing, from about the age of ten, that while the adults mostly retained their pronounced southern accents, my brother and I had already begun to speak in the more neutral tones of the Bay Area. This transplanted church culture was my heritage but not my culture.

Ours was a home in which voices were never raised in anger. Never. This didn't feel like repression then, and it still doesn't. The two loudest sounds were music and laughter. My father played piano, guitar, and French horn, the last of those being the instrument I also chose to take up in school. My brother chose the flute and the guitar. The three of us also liked playing recorders together. My mother hadn't ever taken up an instrument, and it was typical of her modest ways to deprecate her musical abilities in comparison with those of her husband and sons. In truth, she had a lovely soprano voice that made me want to stand beside her whenever we sang hymns at church and at home. And the mirth that still echoes to me across the years was especially infectious at our Sunday dinners. These usually took place around two or three in the afternoon, after we'd changed our clothes from church and fallen in to help my mother with what was always a pretty big production.

Just as the food at our socials hearkened back to similar church events in the South, the heart of my mother's cooking at home was the food she remembered from her own home at the farm in northern Louisiana. Chicken and dumplings, turnip greens, corn bread, rolls and jam from the plum trees in our front yard, deep-dish peach cobbler in season, all washed down with iced tea from the condensation-beaded pitchers stationed on either side of our mahogany dining room table. When guests joined us and a table leaf was swung up to increase the seating space, there was barely room to move around in the small dining area of our Mill Valley home.

As we settled more deeply into the meal, lingering sedately over seconds (no reason not to take another dumpling or two), my father would begin to tell jokes from his endless supply. The talking dog and the skeptical bartender, the tramp tumbling into the freshly dug grave into which another benighted soul had already fallen, the backwoods fellow from Alabama who takes his bride into a hardware store and tries to order lunch, the inherited parrot with the salty vocabulary. They were silly to the point of being ridiculous, but again and again they got us laughing so hard we couldn't stop until we slid out of our chairs and were sitting against the wall beneath the big double window. Which of course just kept the whole group laughing.

Although my father was a more gregarious, performative personality than my more placid and retiring mother, he was like her in never showing a forbidding or angry face to my brother and me as we grew up. I didn't feel the slightest falseness about his self-presentation and was always proud of his charming and entertaining ways. But I did notice occasions when his positive affect was, while still pleasant, kind of odd. He was, in the ways of his Scotch Irish ancestry, remarkably frugal. When we drove across country each summer to visit our relatives in Louisiana and Mississippi, we stayed in some pretty sketchy motels. Lunch was sandwiches packed in a shoebox; supper was hash and potatoes cooked by my mother on a Coleman stove set up on the tailgate of our Pontiac station wagon. Though these were not deluxe tours, I was always struck by my father's exuberant pleasure in simple things. We would check into our $5–a-night room, and Dad would sit down on the mattress of one of our beds and, more often than not, pat it and say: "Feel that mattress. That's what I would call a good, firm one." Or we'd indulge ourselves in ice-cream cones and he'd say: "Taste that ice-cream! So sweet and so cold!" These were not jokes, and nobody laughed. They felt to me as a child like good things to say, even if not exactly necessary.

Only toward the very end of my father's life did I get a feeling for where such determined affirmation of simple pleasures might have come from. It wasn't, I concluded, from his hardscrabble upbringing by a harsh mother in Gulf Coast Mississippi. Rather, his outlook and affect were inseparable from the nightmare of World War II. After graduating from the Baptist Seminary in Louisville, he had joined the 82nd Airborne Division as the first paratrooper chaplain in the army. As a small child in New Orleans in the early 1950s I would ask him about the war, since stories of soldiers' experiences were so prominent in magazines like *Reader's Digest* and *Saturday Evening Post*. But that was the one place in my relationship with Dad where I found a firmly closed door. Shortly before his illness and death in 1994 he gave a long interview to an oral history project and I learned that he was at Omaha Beach on D-Day, that he had broken his leg in a training jump at night in England and thus arrived not by air but in an amphibious landing craft, as in *Saving Private Ryan*, that the Catholic chaplain and graves' registration officer were both killed in the assault, and that his role in the days and weeks following the invasion was to walk the beach and identify the remains of his fallen comrades. I also learned that he had a breakdown after this experience, was shipped to an army facility in France for a couple of weeks, and then was back in his unit for the Battle of the Bulge, when he took a piece of shrapnel through his side and out his back. That explained the wide, livid scars I'd inspected quietly on family trips to go swimming at Lake Ponchartrain. Throughout much of his time in France, too, he was the surgeon's assistant for amputations and other battlefield operations.

It was a bloody immersion for a gentle Sunday School boy who liked to sing, and like many a combat veteran he turned the page when he came home to my mother and Lyn, the almost three-year-old son he'd never met. What could he have said, and who would have understood? For him, I now believe, the choice was a stark one between living in the darkness and turning away from it. Hence his stylized but engaging and interesting exclamations while patting the mattress and tasting the ice cream. He chose to live. I'm also certain Dad's combination of devoutness and religious open-mindedness, along with his highly sympathetic responses to such a wide variety of people, was strengthened by the cataclysm of his early manhood. In a world of such horrible suffering, kindness and forbearance made the most sense to him.

Northern California felt to both of my parents like a refreshing opening, and their attitude briskly ushered Lyn and me, too, into a new world. In Louisiana I had gone to segregated public schools and had little significant contact with African Americans. In California I stepped into a world that was more pluralistic and dynamic. I remember coming home from third grade in Albany, California, with the "N word" on my lips and having both my parents sit me down immediately to explain that our family never used such language under any circumstances. Their own unusual degree of seriousness made this a sobering moment for me, and I have always been grateful to my parents for not letting the occasion slide. Later in that same year a Sunday School teacher had taken special pains to impress us all with our duty to bring others to Christ, in fulfillment of the Great Commission. So I set off to school one Monday determined to evangelize Hal, my Jewish best friend. My mother headed me off at the door when she saw the bible under my arm and told me to leave it at home; Hal had his own religion, and what I had been led to view as a loving action toward him would simply destroy our friendship.

Though such moments of guidance within the family were invisible to a rising group of would-be censors, other aspects of my parents' aerated religious lives were less under wraps. My father's teaching at the seminary, with its warm appreciation of the broader world of process-thought, came to the attention of certain denominational politicians. One statewide publication accused him of "not having a personal devil." I remember Dad laughing about this, which suggested to me that the accusation may have been true. My mild-mannered mother even came in for criticism by the same types after she was ordained as a deacon at the Tiburon Baptist Church. With the apron she always wore around the house and her devotion to the world of kitchen and garden, she was an unlikely champion for feminism. But she calmly pointed out the biblical warrant for women deacons, in such early Christian figures as Dorcas. Though after heading off to

Pomona College I'd begun to drift away from my own affiliation with the Baptists, I felt angry about having people of my parents' character come in for criticism by such hypocrites and boobs. For their part, though, Mom and Dad never spoke harshly about those who impugned their motives. With friends from their early days at LSU and Louisville, they quietly established an escrow fund so that their lifelong double tithing could continue to go toward socially progressive initiatives within the Southern Baptist Convention. And they continued to delight in their own church and in their deep experience of a Bible-based faith.

What has been borne in on me through moving back and forth between Matthew's Passion and the lives of my parents is the perpetual need for dialogue between tenderness and resolve. This is true both in reading the Bible and in trying to participate in the major crises of one's time on earth. I believe that climate destabilization caused by overly consumptive and wasteful societies like our own is in fact the crucial religious challenge facing the world now. It imposes the gravest suffering on the most vulnerable human populations; it disrupts natural systems on which so many species beyond our own depend for their existence; it blights the beauty of our blue-green world. But for all of us who live in the economically developed world there is no way to shunt the blame onto oil-company executives or conservative politicians. With relation to climate change, middle-class citizens of the West, as of the industrialized nations of East Asia, are all goats. Our most appropriate and constructive response will be a combination of repentance and determination—both to bend our nations' policies in the direction of renewable energy and fairness and to transform our own household practices toward mindfulness and restraint.

When Peter realized, at the end of Matthew 26, that he had betrayed Jesus for the third time, "he went out and wept bitterly." Repentance and renewal are similarly called for now by people like myself whose way of life reflects the assumptions of our greedy and consumptive society. But, as was true for Peter, such transformation will only become real when enacted, both in our roles as citizens and in our personal practice. Such an urgent call for change is at the core of Matthew's depiction of the Passion as it was for that long-ago revival in Bastrop. Because of my parents' examples, though, I believe that we can pursue fundamental change without falling into the divisiveness and anger expressed by Matthew or the manipulation and hysteria of that tent meeting. In addition to *agapé*, another word from the Greek New Testament that my father liked to reflect on was *hamartía*. This term, which is translated as "sin," is generally taken to refer to a shameful moral infraction. But Dad liked to point to its original connection with an archery target, so that a more accurate meaning would therefore be "missing the mark." A moment of crisis such as the present one requires us, collectively and individually, to aim in a different direction. We may do so more effectively, however, if instead of squandering too much of our energy berating others or ourselves we advance together in mutual affection and encouragement.

2

Fifteen Stations in the Passion
According to Mark

JULIA ALVAREZ

As a young Catholic girl, one of my favorite devotions was saying the Stations of the Cross. The exercise appealed to me, a restless church-bound girl, because unlike other forms of prayers—in which we knelt before an image, stationary, gazing on passively—the Stations of the Cross involved actual movement. We walked from station to station, stood and contemplated, knelt and prayed, before moving on. There were fourteen stations in all, fourteen earmarked places in the Passion of Jesus where the suffering spilled over. These particular moments in the Passion were depicted on the walls of most Catholic churches, seven on each side, all the way from the altar down to the front entrance and then back up the other side to the altar. What we were doing, in fact, was accompanying Jesus on his way to Calvary. Almost two thousand years after his death, we were not going to leave him to suffer all by himself again.

But I became especially fascinated with the stations as a young immigrant girl when we moved to a parish in Queens, New York, that had a small, woodsy grove where one could say the Stations of the Cross outdoors.

The church itself was a huge warehouse of a building surrounded by an endless parking lot that stretched all the way to the playground of the Catholic school my sisters and I were attending. To one side of this parking lot, at the margins of the church property, lay the shady grove, which was mostly unused. The grass between the stations was occasionally mowed; the bird droppings hosed off in the summer. In the winter no one remembered to shovel the walk or dust the snow off the stones. Indoors, warm and cozy, hung the elegant, framed stations with nearby pews for comfortable kneeling in prayer. Since the grove was somewhat secluded and heavily shaded, I felt a pang of fear as I climbed the steps through a break in the bedraggled bushes. What if a mugger might be crouching behind *Jesus is helped by Simon* (5th station) or *Jesus is stripped of his garments* (10th station) who would relieve me of my garments and make me undergo suffering—which was really much better endured in the spirit than in the flesh.

Inside the garden a stone path wound round in a circle marked by the fourteen stations, beginning with the first depicting *Jesus being condemned to death*. Then came *Jesus bearing his cross*, *Jesus falling the first time*, and one of my favorites, the fourth, *Jesus meeting his mother*. Two stations later *Jesus meets Veronica*, another favorite, and this connection with women continued at the eighth station, in which *Jesus speaks to the women*. Through the trees, across the parking lot, inside the church, his back to the congregation (this was 1962, pre–Second Vatican Council's changes), surrounded by male attendants and altar boys, the priest intoned the mass.

But out here in the deserted garden there was female access to the Christ being worshiped indoors. Those tender moments—a mother weeping at the sight of her beaten, broken son; a young woman wiping the blood, sweat, and tears from his suffering face; a group of desolate women reaching toward their bruised and abused teacher who is bearing the cross on which he will shortly be put to death—stirred me. I lingered before these images and reached to dust the snow from Jesus' anguished face much as Veronica had done with her veil.

Despite my racing heart, I loved saying the stations in this dark and gloomy spot, which, I was convinced, was what the Garden of Gethsemane must have been like. Perhaps also, having recently fled the dictatorship of Trujillo in the Dominican Republic, dazed and traumatized by the months of terror that had preceded our exodus, I now had some glancing acquaintance with the visceral fear and loss that brimmed over in those fourteen awful moments. As my young faith began to be tested and my lapsing from the Catholicism of my childhood began, this was one place I felt close to what I've since learned the Passion story is all about.

Forty-five years later, returning to contemplate the Passion as presented in the Gospel of Mark, I'm immediately struck by the absence of women in his account of Christ's suffering on the way to Calvary. But if this is true of the Passion itself, Mark frames his account with two incidents of women ministering or attempting to minister to the physical body of Christ. Before the suffering starts, there is the woman in Bethany who pours her alabaster jar of expensive ointment over Jesus' head despite the protests of some guests who think this is a waste of money. After Christ utters his last cry and dies, the evangelist mentions that "there were women watching from a distance," the very same women who will later go to his tomb to anoint him, only to find him gone. Instead, a young man in a white robe will tell them what those wonderful angels in Bethlehem thirty-three years earlier told the poor shepherds, *Do not be afraid.* But of course, they are terrified, just as I was terrified every time I rounded the grove and spied a lengthening shadow as the sun went behind a cloud, just as my parents had been terrified each time the black Volkswagens of the secret police climbed up our driveway and surrounded our house at night. The spirit is willing but the flesh is weak, hungry, in pain, tired, and terrified. Who wouldn't bolt, betray, break, or emigrate when the horror shows up in their own lives?

That is why Mark, the grimmest of the evangelists, frames the Passion with these two instances of female tenderness—the only consolation we will get from him—as if to contain it. "Mankind cannot bear very much reality," as T. S. Eliot reminds us in the *Four Quartets.* Perhaps that is why in reading Mark's Passion, I revert to that old favorite framework of the Stations of the Cross: a way to take in the suffering in small "sound bites" because truly we cannot bear this horrible story in its full impact.

And so, I propose to stop at fifteen moments in the Passion of Mark. These are not the traditional stations I knew as a girl, many of which are not moments in Mark anyhow—all the encounters with women I mentioned above, for example. They are instead moments where I feel the brimming over of feeling or insight in reading the text, places where the eye lingers, or the hand absently reaches out to stroke the page. How to bear so much painful reality? Stations, like stories, offer a way to parcel out and mitigate the heart of darkness, string through the labyrinth of suffering that breaks us all, every last one of us, if we are to believe the Passion according to Mark.

Station One

Jesus is anointed by the woman at Bethany. Some begrudge this "waste."

If by the Passion we mean the suffering of Jesus, it begins here in what is seemingly the lull before the storm. Be watchful, he has cautioned in the chapter preceding this account of his dinner in Bethany. Be watchful, lest the lord of the house come suddenly and find you sleeping. The dread in his own heart must be kicking in. Beyond the warm circle of friendship at this table, a plot is afoot; the high priests and scribes are looking for a way to kill him.

But here in Bethany, for this evening, recounted in Mark 14, friends are gathered together, affirming fellowship, a supper prefiguring the last supper. The lamps are lit, the women come in and out to check on what is needed; the smells of cooking waft in from the yard; the soft murmur of conversation. For the moment violence and betrayal seem far away. In one of those expansive gestures of fond devotion, an unidentified woman pours "an alabaster jar of very costly ointment of nard" on Jesus' head. How sweet to feel a soft hand in his hair as he braces himself for the end!

But his friends and supporters begrudge the gesture, even calculating how much money has been wasted: "more than three hundred denarii." Money that might instead be given to the poor, they point out. This is the mantle of righteous goodness that cloaks a stingy soul. Have they factored into their calculations that he is about to sacrifice his only life, worth a lot more? It has to be a needle in the heart to be faced with this smallness of spirit just at the moment when Jesus must yearn for evidence that he is leaving behind strong, big-hearted disciples and followers who can embody the spirit of his life.

It's also a sneaky smallness. For the disciples do not grumble openly about the gesture. They scold the woman. But Jesus defends her, not as one would expect, by taking up the question of his deserving. After all, as their Messiah, isn't he entitled to much more than three hundred denarii worth of perfume? But to respond in this way would be to trade in their currency, to embrace their mentality of nickel-and-diming in order to prove his worth. Instead, he asks simply, "Why do you trouble her? She has performed a good service for me." Her glorious, tender gesture shows more vision than their righteous calculations. This is the anointment he won't be getting at his death. For later, when the women come to his tomb to anoint him, they will not find him there.

In fact, this woman without a name has seen something his trained disciples have missed. She has recognized the Messiah, a title that, after all, means "the anointed one." In Mark, these sideline figures without names or credentials are often the ones who surprise us.

Be watchful, he has told them, but they are already asleep. They have not been transformed, after all. This is the first of many betrayals to come.

Station Two

The Last Supper. One who dips into the dish with Jesus
will betray him.

Here is another supper, this one more staged.

First, two apostles are sent ahead to procure the room by means of instructions that sound a bit like a treasure hunt: "Go into the city, and a man carrying a jar of water will meet you [instead of a woman? water instead of expensive perfume, three hundred denarii's worth?]; follow him, and wherever he enters, say to the owner of the house, 'The Teacher asks, Where is my guest room where I may eat Passover with my disciples?'"These are the kind of instructions the apostles relish—doable deeds, details falling in place, an in-group feel to the whole production. Self-important little men moving and shaking. The arrangements click into place. Just like the boss said.

And so, that night, they sit down at the table, a tight fraternity "in the know," with seeming power to bring about results. Instead, they hear shocking news. Jesus says, "One of you will betray me."They respond not with concern for the victim, Jesus, but for themselves. "Surely, not I?" The response recalls Lady Macbeth's exclamation upon hearing that her guest, King Duncan, has been murdered during the night. "What, in our house?" The king's death is not the tragedy but the fact that it should happen under her roof. "Too cruel anywhere," Banquo reminds her.

When the apostles persist in wanting to know who it is, Jesus responds that his betrayer is "one who is dipping bread into the bowl with me." It is one thing to betray a stranger, or acquaintance, or even a friend. But the poignancy is brought home with this detail. Jesus' betrayer is someone who is intimate with him. They don't just eat; they eat from the very same dish.

My husband, who worked in an eye hospital in the West Bank for a year, tells how occasionally he would be invited out to the countryside by a grateful patient to eat a meal at a tribal household. He was struck by the intimacy of eating together. It was not just a shared meal, each one serving himself on his separate plate.

Everyone was actually eating from the same plate. "You're exchanging body fluids," he explains it. Back in my own past, I met an Amish family who was "shunning" a daughter who had married outside the faith. The young woman could visit the household but never again would she be allowed to eat at its table. In our fast-food nation, we tend to forget that eating together is an intimate act—a sacred, if secular, sacrament.

One who is dipping bread into the bowl with me. The devil is in the details. Betrayal is not just a momentary act but also a betrayal of all the intimacies we have shared. How much more painful is that larger loss. It were better for Judas if he had never been born, even if he is helping bring about a prophecy.

But wait. The one who will betray him, Jesus says, is one who dips into the bowl with him. Aren't they all at the table, presumably eating and dipping into the dish with him? They are right to ask, *Surely, not I?* The answer is yes. All of them will betray him before the night is out.

What strikes me is what follows this announcement. The one who will betray him is not exposed and cast out. In fact, he, too, is given the bread and wine of that first communion. For Judas, it must be astonishing; he has been found out, but he has not been cast out. This is a new, more expansive love than any one of them could have dreamed up or is yet capable of.

Station Three

*Jesus tells his disciples they will all fail him. Peter protests
very forcefully.*

But Peter is absolutely sure that he will not betray his Lord. Didn't Jesus himself say that Peter is the rock on which the church will be built? He is ready to die for Jesus, he insists with passionate intensity, and hearing him say so, the others fall in.

They mean it. They really do. And they are right to affirm "the better angels of their nature," to quote Abraham Lincoln. What is best in us must be given voice or it ceases to exist. Even in as dark a book as Cormac McCarthy's novel *The Road*, where the world is destroyed and the few survivors are tooth and nail, hunting each other down, the boy who travels with his father toward a destination never named keeps asking his dad, "We're the good guys, right? The keepers of the light." We have to fan those dying embers—if for no other reason than to keep alive in ourselves the memory of that saving grace.

Perhaps it's as simple as that, why Jesus keeps bringing up the fact of his betrayal again and again. It gives the apostles the opportunity to posit their loyalty, their love for him. To keep the embers of faith alive, embers that might later flare into flames of faith and love. Especially when the apostles remember that Jesus knew that they would fail him, but still he kept them close. He saw the worst devils of their nature and still—as with Judas at the last supper—he did not throw them off.

But his constant mention of betrayal is also one of many reminders in Mark that Jesus is flesh and blood; he is suffering like any man. It is a pebble in his shoe, a bump he needs to keep going over. These intimates who break bread with him and have followed him for years will betray him.

Jesus knows the truth and says so, stripping away feel-good promises, lies we tell others and ourselves. It is part and parcel of his refusal later to take the drug of wine mixed with myrrh that might blunt the agony of being nailed to a cross. He refuses to operate on any other level than the truth about himself and others. We must see things for what they are. We must see into our hearts of darkness even as we affirm that we are children of the light.

Station Four

Jesus calls out, "Abba, Father . . . remove this cup from me."

Jesus is shuddering, shaken, distressed. "I am deeply grieved, even to death," he confesses to the three apostles he has chosen to accompany him. He throws himself on the ground. This is powerful, visceral, physical fear. Jesus is overcome.

The anticipation of suffering can break a person. The Buddhists call it the second arrow. The first is the pain itself, but the second is the mental anguishing over the pain. My uncle, who was arrested by the secret police and survived six months in the torture prisons in the Dominican Republic, later recalled that the worst torture was the constant dread, not knowing what would happen, but imagining the worse.

And Jesus knows what will happen. He has been talking about it constantly. But now that the hour has almost come, he loses heart. "Abba!" he cries out. "Father!" This is the only place in Mark's Gospel where Jesus addresses God by calling him Father. It is the cry of a terrified child.

This terrified cry is followed so quickly by Jesus' bowing to his fate that it's easy to think, that's right, he *is* the Son of God. He knows better. But part of being a terrified child is to lose all sense of agency. "Yet, not what I want, but what you want." This utterance is scarier than we think, a total surrender of his own power. Do with me as you will. Is this something we want to hear from a leader?

Of course not. We want him to "rage, rage against the dying of the light," as Dylan Thomas urges his own dying father. Our leaders should be powerful people who put up a fight. They should "not go gentle into that good night." Why would an evangelist show Jesus in such a vulnerable light? Doesn't he want to round up converts, believers? Furthermore, how does Mark even know what Jesus prays when no one is watching, when no one will stay up with him?

Unlike the sleeping disciples, Mark is staying awake, and as we read his words, so are we. This is the good news of the Gospel, an awful one to be sure. Robert Desnos, the surrealist French poet who died in a concentration camp, wrote that the task of being a human being is not only to be one's self, but to become each one. Through an act of the imagination, which some call faith, we *become* this suffering man.

But what a time to become Jesus—at his worst, most broken moment!

Station Five
Jesus asks his apostles to stay up with him. Three times he wakes them, and three times they fall asleep.

What else can Jesus ask for at this moment of utter terror but the solace of friendship, human warmth and company? "Sit here while I pray."

He then selects three of them, Peter, James, and John, to form yet another ring of protection and company. "Remain here, and keep awake."

In anguish after trying to pray, Jesus goes back to find them all sleeping—including the very same Peter who minutes earlier protested that he would die for his friend. It is no accident that Mark has Jesus single him out with the question, "Simon, are you asleep?"

Simon? Earlier, when Jesus had established the Twelve, he had renamed Simon, Peter. A new name for a new life. But by calling him by his old name, Jesus lets us understand that Simon has not been changed into Peter, after all.

Three times, or actually five, counting the two earlier instances in this same passage, Jesus finds all of his apostles asleep. Be watchful and wakeful, he has been telling them in preparation for this moment. But even as he chides them, he understands that they really mean to be better. "The spirit is eager, but the flesh is weak." Years ago when I was teaching poetry in the schools, a young student in tenth grade, Katie, wrote this poem:

> Why is it
> I reach for the stars
> but I never make it
> past the front door?

Katie, girl, I wanted to say, welcome to the human condition. We're all torn among our daily responsibilities, our very real creaturely needs, our limitations, and our far-reaching, star-catching dreams. To give up on that struggle is to become a diminished person, flesh without a chance of ever becoming spirit.

Interestingly, this summons to wake up is a strain in many religions. Rumi, the Sufi poet, urges us, "Do not go back to sleep." Lord Krishna rallies the sleepy Arjuna to arise and join the fray of an awakened life. One of my favorite stories of the Buddha tells how, after he becomes famous, many learned men come to visit him trying to figure out who exactly Buddha is.

"Buddha, are you a god?" they ask him.

"No, I am not a god," the Buddha replies.

"So are you a saint?" they ask.

"No," the Buddha replies, "I am not a saint."

Finally they ask, "So what are you, Buddha?"

And the Buddha says, "I am awake."

We are not gods or saints. The word has to be made flesh. Not just the eager spirit, but also the weary flesh; it takes both to be awake.

The final time Jesus wakes them, it is already too late. The hour has come. His betrayer is near. Had they kept watch, they might have warned him. There might have been a little window in there to get away, to avoid being seized in the middle of the night. In our Latin American dictatorships, late-night squads would haul off the suspect, who would disappear without a trace. A new term entered our vocabulary, *to be disappeared*. As if he had never been born. The deepest sleep of all, one that Jesus warned would be the legacy of the man who betrays him.

It turns out that while Jesus' followers slept, others have stayed awake, others who come under the cover of darkness wanting to do away with Jesus as if he had never been born. This is an addendum to the Buddha story. It turns out it is not enough to be awake. To what end do we put our wakefulness? In "Ars Poetica," Czselaw Milosz recognizes that the power of poetry can be used for good and bad purposes:

> The purpose of poetry is to remind us
> how difficult it is to remain just one person,
> for our house is open, there are no keys in the
>   doors,
> and invisible guests come in and out at will.

What I'm saying here is not, I agree, poetry,
as poems should be written rarely and reluc-
            tantly,
under unbearable duress and only with the hope
that good spirits, not evil ones, choose us for
            their instrument.

We must hope and pray that our wakefulness is in the service
of what is good and just. "Lord, make me an instrument of thy
peace," begins that old prayer attributed to Saint Francis of Assisi.
Instruments of peace in the wrong hands can become weapons of
mass destruction. In our time we have seen a president transform
a whole nation into the latter.

Station Six

Judas betrays Jesus. "Rabbi!" he greets him and kisses him.

Here is the man who should never have been born. Judas betrays
Jesus, addressing him as Rabbi, giving him a kiss. This sharpens
the edge of betrayal—achieving it by the very gestures that signal
intimacy and trust, gestures like the earlier one at the table, dipping into the same bowl with Jesus. A coward's way.

Why does Judas betray Jesus? Mark never explains. The high
priests promise to give Judas money, but this reward is only
mentioned after he has gone to them, and quickly passed over.
But that does not seem to have been his motivation. To be able to
explain a horrible deed with a motive, however flimsy, reduces
the horror. But Mark's silence on the matter is like Iago's silence
when Othello asks him why he has "thus ensnared my soul and
body?" A silence that is eerie, inhuman.

It would be more bearable to hear an excuse, however flawed. Instead, Judas disappears from the narrative with that kiss. It is odd that he does not follow through on his betrayal by being part of the rigged-up proceedings that are about to take place in the high priest's house. Why is he not one of the witnesses who are brought in to give false testimony? Is he just a pawn of the plot, used to fulfill a prophecy?

Jesus does not respond to the kiss or greeting of "Rabbi!" He matches Judas's silence with his own. So does Mark. As if Judas were not before him, as if indeed he had never been born.

Station Seven

Jesus' supporter draws a sword and cuts off the ear of the slave of the high priest.

Jesus is seized and bound, but he does not put up a struggle. Instead, one of his supporters starts the violence. Again, have they learned nothing from him?

"Have you come out with swords and clubs to arrest me as though I were a bandit?" Jesus accuses his accusers. In fact, he will be crucified with two robbers, as if he were a common criminal. But he refuses to fight back or to hide or to flee. Now begins the great unveiling of who he is. And the unveiling of his accusers: they are cowards who could have seized him at any time, openly, in broad daylight. Instead, they come for him under the cover of night.

But his supporters are similarly cowardly. Whom do they strike? The slave of the high priest. The old Marxist saw: the boss kicks the worker, the worker goes home and kicks his wife, his wife kicks the child, and the child kicks the dog.

Jesus nips the violence in the bud. There will be no fighting. It is enough. From here on, Jesus surrenders himself to what is coming. He grows quieter and quieter as the Passion proceeds. "Have you no answer?" the high priest asks him in the ensuing interrogation that night. "Have you no answer?" Pilate asks the following day.

Violence is a violation of the effort to communicate. There are no answers in this kind of a world.

Station Eight

A certain young man who had been following him is seized and he flees naked, leaving his linen garment behind.

Even in the grimmest of Shakespeare's tragedies there are moments of comic relief: the drunken porter in *Macbeth*, the fool in *King Lear*.

Who is this fellow? Why is he wearing only a linen garment over his bare skin? It is a chilly night. A little later, Peter will be warming himself in front of a fire in the courtyard of the high priest's house.

This fellow has been following Jesus, making a show of his allegiance, like spiritual groupies who showcase their faith, dressed in ashes and sackcloth, lying on a bed of nails. But when the moment comes, the young devotee turns on his heels, terrified, leaving his garment behind!

This moment recalls the stripping away by Jesus of Peter's promises and avowals, a stripping that will continue throughout the Passion until that linen garment reappears as the shroud in which Joseph of Arimathea will wrap the body of Jesus. And that young man will be recalled in the young man sitting inside the tomb wearing a white robe. None of us will get away scot free, after all.

Station Nine

The chief priests and the elders and scribes bring forward false witnesses. The proceedings end with the high priest tearing his clothing, condemning Jesus.

Late night, a rigged-up court, a travesty of a legal proceeding; the false witnesses don't agree, the accused won't talk. The high priest condemns the prisoner as a blasphemer and only as an afterthought asks the rest of the council, "What is your decision?"

In fact, "Why do we still need witnesses?" the high priest asks rhetorically, tearing his robe, a stripping we've seen before. But this stripping is not an effort to bring to light some essence or truth. As with other symbols and gestures—the kiss, the dipping into the bowl—this gesture is a show; it smacks of manipulation, a histrionic ploy. This is what it means to live in a fallen world; the very means by which we communicate in order to understand and clarify are corrupted and destroyed.

Why can't this proceeding wait until morning? For the same reason that those who arrested Jesus did not do so openly when he was in the Temple teaching. But is this legal? Mark underscores that "all the chief priests, the elders, and the scribes were assembled." They *all* judged that he deserved death. "The chief priests and the *whole* council." In Mark's Passion there are no dissenting voices, no one of two robbers repenting, no friends at the foot of the cross weeping, no Veronica wiping Christ's face. This is a dark and terrifying world in dire need of salvation.

It does seem amazing that a seventy-one-member council
could be assembled at night during festival time without a single
absence. Did no one go out of town for the holiday? Of course,
this smacks of a setup, albeit a sloppy one; those false witnesses
should have been coached more carefully so their testimony
would agree. But Mark follows this death verdict by "all" with
the smaller denomination of only "some" who mock him. Later,
Joseph of Arimathea, "a respected member of the council, who
was also himself waiting expectantly for the kingdom of God,"
takes courage to go to Pilate to ask for the body of Jesus to bury.
Was he one of the "all" assembled at the high priest's house,
swept up by the mob mentality we'll see later at Pilate's house,
that juggernaut that destroys individual conscience? Did Joseph
see the light only after an internal cock crowed and he realized
what he had done? I'm sure some in that room were too afraid
to object. Then, too, it's important to remember that often those
we call evil consider themselves just. They, too, are swept up with
the righteousness of their cause. That is why we hope and pray
that good spirits, not evil ones, choose us for their instrument.

As for the proceedings themselves, Jesus does not respond
to the first accusation that is made, albeit by false, contradic-
tory witnesses. He is accused of saying that he will destroy
the Temple made with hands and build another not made with
hands, a wacky claim that should have landed him in whatever
equivalent there was to a loony bin, not in the Place of the Skull.
From early on in his ministry Jesus has made clear to his apostles
and followers that he is not interested in temporal, ecclesiastical
power—temples made with hands. When the council cannot
nail him on that one, the high priest asks him if he is the Christ,
the son of the Blessed One. Interestingly enough, the question
is not, as with the first accusation, "Do you say that you are the

Christ?" Instead, he is asked, "Are you the Messiah?" And Jesus replies, "I am."

Jesus has unveiled himself before his accusers. Placed beside the figure of the high priest tearing his clothing in a show of rage, we are shown the difference between a temple made with hands and one made without hands.

Station Ten

Peter denies knowing Jesus three times. The cock crows. He remembers Jesus' words and throws himself down and cries.

All the other disciples have deserted Jesus, but Peter follows him into the courtyard of the high priest. He must be given credit for that. He is less a coward than the rest of us.

But he is surrounded. He has no one to help bolster his courage. Or rather, there is someone. Mark juxtaposes Peter's denial to Jesus' open declaration before the entire council. But Peter has reverted back to Simon, still fast asleep in an internal Garden of Gethsemane.

When the cock crows upon his third denial, Peter remembers Jesus' prediction about his betrayal and he throws himself down just as Jesus did in the Garden of Gethsemane, a mirroring gesture of true despair. Peter has woken up, meeting Jesus on that ground zero, that broken place.

But Peter will get another chance. In a world where there is forgiveness—unlike this chilly, benighted courtyard—there is always one more cock crow, one more chance to turn again, to find courage, to return to the circle of community, to the love that will not give up on us. In this sense the cock's crow is not an announcement of betrayal but a wakeup call. Jesus will not deny

Peter. No wonder the serving girl recognizes something in Peter, just as the woman with her alabaster jar in Bethany recognized something about Jesus. These sideline figures, as I mentioned before, have an eye for spirit.

If Judas disappears from Mark's Gospel with a kiss, we last see Peter lying on the ground in tears.

This is the rock on which a whole church will be built.

Station Eleven

Jesus is brought before Pilate with the charge that he claims to be King of the Jews. Pilate is unconvinced, but he gives the crowd the choice, Jesus or Barabbas. They choose.

It has been a busy time for the council of the chief priests, the elders, and the scribes. After their late-night proceedings they meet again, now in the light of day. No mention is made of their earlier gathering, so this morning meeting must be the showcase hearing in which Jesus is openly accused, everything above board. Presumably, the witnesses have had a chance to coordinate their conflicting testimonies of the night before and the high priest's wife has mended his torn robes.

Interestingly, though the late-night court condemned Jesus to death, this "whole council" decides to hand Jesus over to Pilate instead. From Pilate's questioning we learn that the charge has been changed to Jesus' claim that he is "the King of the Jews." A savvy political spin to make the authorities nervous, no doubt. The Romans are, after all, occupiers in this country. Think Iraq, think Americans worried about civil war, uprisings, terrorist bombings. And it's festival time, a time of crowds, a time when riots are likely to break out, a good time to release a prisoner, a safety valve to prevent the buildup of resentment from exploding into full revolt. In fact, the prisoner in question, one Barabbas, was imprisoned along with some insurgents during an uprising. Pilate is in a tricky position; he does not want trouble. The entire council shows up at his door, the movers and shakers who can manipulate public opinion. They've brought in someone who is claiming to be the king of this occupied land.

But, come now! *This* is the King of the Jews? By his constant repetition of the phrase, one senses that Pilate is mocking not Christ, but his accusers. This beaten, silent man is hardly insurgent material. Barabbas is by far the more dangerous of the two to the state. King of the Jews? When questioned, Jesus doesn't even try to defend himself. "You say so," he answers the charge. No wonder Pilate is amazed. He knows this poor wreck of a man is innocent. "What evil has he done?" he asks the members of the crowd, as if they are the ones under interrogation. But there is no reasoning with them. The chief priests have stirred them up.

Pilate is trapped. He has offered the crowd a choice. He is an occupier wanting to satisfy the crowd. And so he ends up crucifying an innocent man while remaining technically clear of having condemned him. But later that day, when Joseph of Arimathea comes to ask permission to bury the body, Pilate is again amazed that this King of the Jews would already be dead. He summons the centurion for confirmation. These are the head scratchings of a man in an occupied land, all right. A man unsettled by the day's events. A man unsure of what he has done. *King of the Jews*, he muses over the phrase. "It was they who said so," Pilate can tell himself, passing the buck on to the crowd and the entire council. But Jesus' words were clear, "You say so." The buck stops here, as Peter discovers—on the ground, weeping bitter tears.

Station Twelve

*The whole cohort clothes Jesus in purple, crowns him with
a wreath of thorns, beats him, mocks him as King of the
Jews, then leads him out to be crucified.*

What pleasure is there in humiliating a man who already has a death sentence on his head?

These are soldiers, supposedly disciplined creatures, not the madding crowd outside. Again Mark emphasizes that "the whole cohort" joined in the fun.

"Hail, King of the Jews!" The cruel joke continues. A mock crowning, soldiers going down on their knees.

We look at images from Abu Ghraib and our hearts stop. The torturers are young men and women—they look like students in my classrooms, like local kids we've watched grow up, like our own sons and daughters.

They are stacking up naked men in a human pyramid, climbing on them, giving the camera a thumbs up, grinning. Why on earth would they want to record this disgusting moment?

A young woman is hauling a naked man on a leash, his hands tied behind his back. A young man is taunting a kneeling man with an attack dog. A prisoner, a black hood over his head, stands on a box, his genitals wired for electric shocks. This is not interrogation justified by an urgent need to save innocent lives. This is glee at participating in the breaking and the suffering of another human being.

In his book *Unspeakable Acts, Ordinary People: The Dynamics of Torture* John Conroy writes that torturers are ordinary people, most of them decent folks obeying authority. *King of the Jews!* The taunt echoes down from the chambers of the powerful council members to the servants in the courtyard. From Pilate, the governor, to the soldiers who lead Jesus inside the official residence and call up the whole cohort. *King of the Jews!* They echo. Evil is infectious, Conroy concludes. Torturers are ordinary people, many of them relying on the moral leadership of higher ups.

And Mark wants us to see this. He slows down the action. Sentence after breathless sentence is a lash stroke, as if by reading the account, we are both participating in and enduring the humiliation: "And they began saluting him. . . . And they struck his head with a reed. . . . After mocking him . . . they led him out to crucify him."

Mark does not turn away. "I am a human being," Terence, the Roman slave and playwright, wrote. "Nothing human is alien to me." In the Passion according to Mark, we are being forced to acknowledge the horrors inside our own military, our own country, our own religion, our own heart. It's as if those sentences were breaking us down as well, as if we, too, have to end up with Peter, weeping on the ground over our own inhumanity to one another.

Station Thirteen

Jesus is led away to Golgotha to be crucified. . . . Simon of Cyrene is impressed to carry the cross. . . . And Jesus is offered wine mixed with myrrh. . . . And his clothes are divided. . . . Then he is crucified.

The lash strokes continue, most sentences beginning with the conjunction *and,* just when we thought we could bear no more.

Certainly Jesus is faltering under the weight of so much abuse. He can't carry his own cross anymore. A certain Simon of Cyrene is *impressed* to carry it, enlisted by force, a draft of sorts. Simon is coming in from the country; perhaps he has been out working in the fields, not part of the festival crowd. He is an outsider to the action so far, someone presumably known to Mark's readers as the father of Alexander and Rufus—just as later, one of the women who is watching the crucifixion from a distance is identified as Mary, the mother of James the Lesser and Joses.

Why does Mark give us this bit of genealogy at this point in the narrative? He knows the deeds he is describing are cruel and horrible. We, his readers, are beginning to falter under the weight of so much violence. Perhaps this account is too exaggerated? So, Mark offers us living proof, a witness, a way to connect us to the story at a point where we want to back away. Any doubts? Go ask Alexander and Rufus what their father saw.

Was Simon's life utterly changed by this encounter? Did he pass on this story to his two sons, who seem to have become part of the community of readers Mark is addressing in his Gospel? Simon is from Cyrene, a city in North Africa. Much has been made of this, Simon being considered an African, the first black saint, although at the time of Christ, Cyrene was a Roman city and former Greek colony, not an African nation. Whatever his exact provenance and race, one thing is clear: Simon is not a native of Jerusalem. The outsiders are being let in. The veil of a temple that separates the holy of holies from the *hoi polloi* is definitely being rent.

Jesus is crucified between two robbers, his offense inscribed on the cross: *King of the Jews*. Now those who mock him bring up all the charges we've heard before, including the original one of Jesus saying that he would tear down the Temple in three days as well as his claim that he is King of Israel. Of course, the chief priests have followed the procession up to Golgotha, the Place of the Skull. They taunt Jesus to come down from the cross, and then they will believe him. This is bogus faith that works by signs, makes conditions, needs proof: the casting of demons, the speaking in tongues, the handling of serpents, the drinking of poison—reason enough to reject the spurious ending in which these claims are made for believers, tacked on to "complete" the Gospel of Mark.

Station Fourteen

Darkness descends on the earth. Jesus calls out, "My God, My God, why have you forsaken me?" Jesus utters a last great cry and dies. The veil in the Temple is split in two. A centurion posted across from the crucified Jesus says, "Truly this man was God's Son!"

Jesus is agonizing on the cross. From the sixth hour (noon) to the ninth hour (three in the afternoon), "darkness came over the whole land." The language is reminiscent of Genesis 1. The Temple veil is being torn asunder just as a newborn tears open his mother's birth canal. Here in the Place of the Skull, that ground zero where all is lost, a new world order is about to be born.

Before he dies, Jesus cries out, "Eloi, Eloi, lema sabachthani? My God, my God, why have you forsaken me?" This is the most terrifying moment in Mark's Passion, worse than the anguish in the Garden of Gethsemane, the late-night arrest, the bogus hearing, the beatings, and the torture. Throughout all those ordeals

Jesus' faith remained intact. "Yet not what I want, but what you want," he says, submitting to his Father's will.

But here, Jesus' last intelligible words are a seeming admission that God has abandoned him. It is as if Jesus loses faith. The chief priests and scribes are right: where is God when Jesus needs him? No wonder the later evangelists, Luke and John, report different last words, either intentionally changing Mark's Passion, fearing that the faithful could not bear this much painful reality, or perhaps choosing another among a variety of reports, one more in keeping with the Jesus they want to believe in and promote.

My first encounter with the Passion of Mark was in catechism class. In eighth grade, during Holy Week, Sister Mary Joseph had us read the four evangelists' accounts of the Passion. Saint Mark's version upset me. My hand shot up. *My God, My God, why have you forsaken me?* "Did Jesus stop believing in God?"

"Of course not!" Sister Mary Joseph replied, annoyance straying into her voice. She had me pegged as someone who asked too many questions. Besides, she was racing us toward the resurrection.

Maybe it was my imperfect English? I looked up *forsaken* in the dictionary. "Abandoned," "deserted." The next class my hand went up again. "Why does Jesus think God has abandoned him?"

"It is not God who has abandoned him, it is humanity."

Sister Mary Joseph was right. It was humankind—the chief priests, the crowds, and the Roman soldiers—doing these cruel things to Jesus. But then why didn't Jesus say, "My people, my people, why have you forsaken me?"

I don't remember pursuing this line of questioning with Sister Mary Joseph. I must have caught on that it would not yield happy results. But now, forty-five years later, I'm still puzzled and disturbed by Jesus' last words. And I think Mark wants me to be.

Jesus' last words are terrifying. He is calling out in despair. God has forsaken him, the only way that God can forsake us, through his creation, the cruelty and betrayal of our human family. We ache for other words. But all we will hear from Jesus before he dies is one last great cry, an animal noise of suffering, not phrased and contained in language. The veil is rent in the Temple. We've seen this stripping throughout the Passion of Mark, a breaking down of the old paradigms, the temple made with human hands.

This is a dark and terrifying place to have Jesus' life end.

Or so it would seem. But not for those who stay with the mystery, who see with the eyes of the woman at Bethany or the centurion posted in front of the cross. "Truly," this centurion says, "this man was God's Son!"

What truth has this man has seen? The others at the foot of the cross are trying their experiments with a sponge soaked in vinegar, wondering if Elijah will come. Credulous and clueless, they are still waiting for their miracle to happen. But Mark has posted the centurion here, as if to say to us who see only defeat and hear only despair in this Place of the Skull, look again. There is another way to understand this story.

"My God, my God, why have you forsaken me?"

These are the very words that open Psalm 22, the psalm of the righteous sufferer, calling out to God, "My God, my God, why have you forsaken me? . . . Trouble is near and there is no one to help." In one of my copies of the bible, a commercial edition with a back cover that advises "Where to look in the Bible: WHEN you can't go to sleep, WHEN tempted to do wrong, WHEN business is poor, WHEN you are bored." Psalm 22 is recommended WHEN the whole world seems to be against you. It is a summoning, an incantation that ends with a triumphant vision of God's kingdom on earth:

> All the ends of the earth shall remember
>> and turn to the LORD;
> and all the families of the nations
> shall worship before him.

By reciting the opening words of the psalm at this moment of extreme suffering, Jesus is affirming his faith. In what Mark describes as a "loud cry," which must be hard for a dying man, Jesus proclaims the truth he foretold to the high priests the night before. God and his kingdom will triumph.

But if Jesus is affirming his faith, why doesn't Mark have him finish reciting the psalm, or at the very least, jump to the triumphant ending? Why not eliminate all doubt so we don't have to wonder if this is a proclamation of triumph or an acknowledgment of defeat?

Mark is testing us. Just when we thought that all was lost, the centurion's incredible utterance sends us back to gaze upon this man on the cross. To reconsider Jesus' words. They *are* unfinished. If we want the joyful ending that Psalm 22 promises, it is we who must complete the story.

Beyond this first convert, this amazed centurion, the circle begins to widen. Watching from a distance are the women who have followed Jesus and served him in Galilee, many others who have come up with him to Jerusalem, as well as Joseph of Arimathea, who is also looking for the kingdom of God. A growing congregation, who must take courage and claim the body of the crucified Christ and pass on an amazing story that he is alive.

Station Fifteen

Mary, the Magdalene, and Mary, the mother of James, and
Salome go to Jesus' tomb.

The women "brought spices, so that they might go and anoint him."
They worried about how to push aside the tombstone. "They saw
that the stone . . . had already been rolled back. As they entered
the tomb, they saw a young man, dressed in a white robe, sitting
on the right side; and they were alarmed. But he said to them,
'Do not be afraid; you are looking for Jesus of Nazareth, who was
crucified. He has been raised.'"The women are to tell his disciples,
and Peter, that Jesus will meet them in Galilee, as he had promised.
But the women "fled from the tomb, for terror and amazement had
seized them; and they said nothing to anyone, for they were afraid."

When I was growing up there were only fourteen stations. The
fourteenth and final stop was *Jesus is laid in the tomb*. A gloomy
ending, very much in the spirit of the Passion according to Mark,
who ends his Gospel with three terrified women fleeing from an
empty tomb. "And they said nothing to anyone, for they were
afraid." How can this be a way to conclude a story that purports
to be good news?

The Catholic Church obviously thought it was not a very good
close to the stations. The very year that I discovered the hidden
grove, the Second Vatican Council added a fifteenth station: *Jesus
rises victorious over death*. It was felt that the crucifixion was point-
less without the resurrection. Emphasis should be on the risen
Christ. The faithful needed a happier ending.

A similar impulse in the second century after Christ resulted
in two alternate endings being tacked on to the Gospel of Mark.
Both endings read very much like the conclusion of Psalm 22,

with the promise of God's reign on earth. The longer ending concludes with these words: "And they went out and proclaimed the good news everywhere, while the Lord worked with them and confirmed their message by the signs that accompanied it." The shorter alternate ending is also a heartening affirmation: "Jesus himself sent forth through them, from east to west, the holy and imperishable proclamation of everlasting salvation." As for the question of authenticity, the Catholic Church has declared that these additions are canonically authentic, even though they are not authentic in a literary sense.

But as a writer, I want my authenticity to also be literary. Besides, it seems to me that those who tack on these alternate, upbeat endings are missing Mark's point. Ironically, they are acting in the spirit of the fearful women, afraid to pass on the true message they have heard.

Why are these women so afraid? Why shouldn't they be? Even Jesus' right-hand man, Peter, has denied him. These women have been hovering in the sidelines, powerless, seeing what can happen to those who defy authority. We must not be hard on them, as Jesus reminded his followers concerning the woman at Bethany. They are trying to do a good thing. As they walk to the tomb, they are worrying about how they will move the large stone at the entrance. When they get there, the stone is already rolled back. At this point, they might have run off, afraid. But no, they investigate further.

Inside, they find a young man who is described in words that echo Jesus' words about his resurrection to the council of chief priests on the night before he died:

> "you will see the Son of Man
> seated at the right of the Power
> and 'coming with the clouds of heaven.'"

Here we see a young man in a white robe sitting on the right side of Jesus' tomb. He tells them not to be amazed. He gives them the good news. Jesus has been raised. He asks them to pass on this news to the disciples and to Peter, who is now reinstated with his God-given name. The women flee. They say nothing to anyone, for they are afraid. End of story.

But how can it be the end of the story? After all, *we* know the story. The women must have eventually spoken out. Either that or the risen Jesus met the disciples in Galilee, as he had promised, and there told them the story of the three terrified women. We cannot know what happened, just as we cannot know what it was the centurion saw, but we do know that we have received this story, just as the women received the message from the young man.

Who is this young man in a white robe? Is he an angel? Is he the young follower who fled leaving his garment behind in the hands of one of the council's soldiers? But an even greater amazement than the messenger is his incredible message: Jesus has been raised. This mystery with which Mark ends his Passion leaves us, his readers, struggling to understand, waiting and watching like these women for that moment of faith to seize us so we can pass on this story.

But a story can only go so far. It is not finished until it takes hold in a reader's imagination. A living understanding. The word made flesh. This is a good place to begin—as John does—or to end the good news. Mark's Passion is inconclusive. Like all true stories it washes up on the shores of our understanding, asking nothing less than for us to complete it by changing our lives.

3

My Week of Sorrows

Reading the Gospel of Luke in Jerusalem

STEPHANIE SALDAÑA

I live in Jerusalem, in an old Arab house that stands just outside of the Damascus Gate, on a road that leads to the winding alleys of the four quarters of the Old City where Jesus spent the last days of his life. From the balconies of my house I often look out and watch the hundreds of people entering and leaving the city through that majestic gate each morning: tourists and pilgrims; Muslims heading to the Dome of the Rock to pray; Jews wearing their traditional white prayer shawls and rushing to the Western Wall with bowed heads; Christian pilgrims and clergy on their way to the Church of the Holy Sepulcher, where tradition says that Jesus was crucified, buried, and raised from the dead. On the side of the road street vendors hawk plums and green almonds, fresh sesame bread and prune juice, shoes and umbrellas and branches of wild thyme. Nablus Road, the street my house stands on, leads directly to all three of the holy sites for Islam,

Christianity, and Judaism. I go to sleep at night and awaken on a pipeline to some of the holiest places in the world.

In time I've gotten used to the fact that there are gifts and also heartbreaks involved in living in such a holy city, particularly on my road, which straddles the border between East and West Jerusalem, Arab and Jewish Jerusalem, in a divided and contested landscape. Yet every now and then those gifts and heartbreaks fold into a single, unique, and terrifying moment. One of those moments occurred last spring, when tensions erupted in the Palestinian community over Israeli construction near the Western Wall and the Dome of the Rock, a site held holy by both Muslims and Jews. Soon, rioting broke out in the Old City between Palestinians and Israeli security forces a few minutes away from where I live. Dozens were wounded, and two thousand Israeli police were deployed in expectation of further riots. As the violence threatened to spill beyond the Old City walls and over into the surrounding streets near my house, Israeli soldiers set up a checkpoint one Friday morning a few steps away from my front door, and young men and women in green uniforms and holding guns checked the papers of all of the Palestinians heading to the Old City for their morning prayers, turning away all men under the age of forty-five. I watched from the terrace on our roof as a crowd of Muslim men and teenage boys who had been turned away from their Friday prayers gathered on the street below. Before long, the line of rejected men stretched from the front of our house halfway down the road, in what looked to me like well over a hundred people. Soldiers, who in my experience here are for the most part frightened twenty year olds trying to look tough (though one should never underestimate a twenty year old trying to look tough), set up metal security barriers along the street, armed and ready. I was frightened. The call to prayer rang out from the mosque.

There was a stirring among the crowd. The soldiers eyed them, ready to react to whatever might follow. Then, much to my amazement, I watched as hundreds of men quietly bowed down in unison in the street in front of my home and prayed. Their foreheads touched the ground, dirty from car exhaust and shoes and all of the havoc of daily life, and they blessed it. They rose and then knelt back down again. A man sang out the prayer from the sidewalk. The soldiers looked on in silence. It was one of the most beautiful moments I had ever witnessed in my life, that uncommon blend of blessed submission by a hundred men, and the rare, kind silence on behalf of the soldiers that allowed that moment to happen. After the crowd of men finished, they stood up, cast one last look toward the Old City, then turned and walked home again. I felt tears coming to my eyes.

I walked inside, where my husband, Frederic, was reading the newspaper.

"I want to have a child," I told him.

He didn't ask any questions. He just held me, and for a moment I felt that we truly did live in the holiest city in the world.

Now, it is more than one year later, and my five-month-old son, Joseph, is asleep in his bed in the other room. I have sat down to write about the Passion in the Gospel of Saint Luke. Still, all I keep thinking about is that afternoon, that moment of grace, that brief truce between enemies in the midst of rising violence all around the city, which finally gave me the courage to carry a life inside my womb.

What is passion? Surely, it is a feeling of a strong emotion, love, desire, and yes, also suffering before and in the midst of death. It is the feeling of urgency that took me to the roof that afternoon to watch the events unfolding in the street below, and the same feeling that sent me into my husband's arms. Passion is what moves us most deeply—and what, in turn, moves history. But that the word *passion* should be tied so exclusively to *death* in the Christian lexicon has always felt unnatural to me, as I've always associated passion with life. And I must admit that this is particularly bizarre in writing about the Gospel of Luke. I grew up attending Catholic schools, with all the trappings of plaid uniforms and rosaries and the Stations of the Cross each Lenten season. I sat through lessons on the Gospels every day in religion class for thirteen years. And I can tell you that from the perspective of a young, wide-eyed Catholic schoolgirl, there *was* no Passion, in the brutal, suffering, Mel Gibson sense, in the Gospel of Luke. Each of the Gospel writers had a significant role to play in my life—Matthew, Mark, Luke, and John were not just fictional names, but real living and breathing human beings for me. Mark was the boring Gospel writer, author of the abridged version of the life of Jesus, a historian who knew the facts about Jesus but didn't have the imagination for the details. Matthew was the opposite—his curly haired Jesus was so real and scholarly that, if he had been a priest, he would have surely been Jesuit, and possibly a Latin teacher—a Jesus brimming with parables and wisdom sayings and invariably my teachers' and priests' favorite. The other two Gospel writers were tied very deeply to the holidays, like the favorite uncles we only saw once or twice a year. John was, without a doubt, the Gospel of the Passion. We read John when we meditated on the Stations of the Cross every Friday of Lent, making our way slowly around the walls of the church, plaque by plaque. We followed his text on Good Friday, when students draped sheets over their shoulders like Roman togas and acted out Jesus' flogging on an unfortunate student named

Chris (who, for some reason, volunteered his body each year), the rest of us chanting from the church pews: "Crucify! Crucify!" Here was suffering, in all of its gory detail, Jesus left to die on the Sabbath and then speared through his side! A passion play was even staged downtown in my largely Hispanic hometown of San Antonio, the death of one Jesús de Nazareth followed by my fellow citizens like a Mexican soap opera. Ah, John. What terror! What horrible suffering! Yes, what passion!

But Luke? Luke was nowhere to be found on Good Friday. No, in my childhood Luke only appeared on Christmas. Every Christmas Eve my classmates dressed up in long shepherds' robes and carried staffs in their arms down the main aisle of the church. Young girls fashioned the wings of angels onto the backs of their long white gowns. An eight-year-old boy dressed up as Joseph looked shyly over at Mary, his blushing eight-year-old bride, and they knelt together in front of a manger holding a fragile (for even then we knew he was fragile) baby boy. Then a student from the eighth grade stood in his starched white dress shirt and solemnly opened the Gospel of Luke before reading the words of an angel: "Do not be afraid; for see—I am bringing you good news of great joy for all the people; to you is born this day in the city of David a Savior, who is the Messiah, the Lord. This will be a sign for you: you will find a child wrapped in bands of cloth and lying in a manger."

Sure enough, the eight-year-old couple held up the swaddled figure of the baby Jesus for all of us to see. We, in all of our childhood innocence, gasped. A child was born! The angel had spoken the truth! Now *that* was Luke. We didn't hear from him again for months, until he turned up after the resurrection to tell us that the tomb was empty and that Jesus had risen—indeed, that he was born again. Being born—that was Luke's business.

That is why his Gospel began with the miraculous pregnancy of Elizabeth and *then* that of Mary, as if just one birth wasn't enough to satiate his thirst for the subject. If Luke had a single *passion*, then it was surely that.

Yet here I am in the thirty-first year of my life, oddly close to the age of Jesus when he was crucified (for who thought that was possible in my childhood!), and living in the city in which he was killed. I am a mother now, and plagued by questions far different than those that must have preoccupied my mind when I read the Gospels in my childhood—not just about the meaning of my son's birth, but about the troubled world I have brought my child into to live. I write this from a house, on a street, in the heart of one of the most divided cities in the world, during a time of war. And as I reread the Gospel of Luke for the first time in many years, I can't help but notice the warning given by Simeon to Mary, the mother of Jesus, after her son is born: "This child is destined for the falling and the rising of many in Israel, and to be a sign that will be opposed so that the inner thoughts of many will be revealed—and a sword will pierce your own soul too."

A sword will pierce your own soul too. This is the story embedded within that story of birth that I never had to think about as a child. Not simply what we gain by Jesus' birth, but also what we will have to lose.

For, it turns out, another passionate story lies buried within the Gospel of Luke even from the opening pages—the story of a child who grows into a man and is put to death—though I have avoided this part of his tale until now. So I have decided to spend the rest of the week meditating on the Passion in the Gospel of Luke a little bit each day, revisiting the text in light of the city I live in and the son to whom I have just given birth. Luke, I hope, would have appreciated this method—for the form of his narrative means that, like a talisman worn against our heart, we carry the story of birth through everything else that follows—no matter how terrible. And though I never knew it as a child, now I understand that things *are* terrible from the very beginning of Luke's story. After all, he opens his story with the line: *In the days of King Herod of Judea* . . . It is a bit like beginning a fairy tale: *Once upon a terrible time* . . . And a child is born into this.

Monday

Today as I read, sirens wail outside of my window, a fitting subtext for a morning spent with the Passion. I open my English/Arabic Bible and turn to the last half of Luke's Gospel, pausing at Palm Sunday, when Jesus leaves Bethany and approaches Jerusalem over the Mount of Olives for the last time before his death. *As he was now approaching the path down from the Mount of Olives,* Luke says. I know the road well, for it exists even to this day.

Why begin here, when the Passion story usually begins when Jesus is arrested and sentenced to death much later in the week? Perhaps it is only because I live here, but I can't help but notice that Luke's Passion is intimately bound not only to *time* but also to *place*—in his case, to the city of Jerusalem. Jerusalem is the city where Jesus comes to die. He cannot die anywhere else. For that reason Jesus' entrance to the city marks the beginning of a new movement in the Gospel, possessing all of the dramatic tension of a classic epic, in which the hero returns home at the end finally to avenge a terrible betrayal. Luke prepares us for the gravity of the moment when Jesus is still teaching in the Galilee, and the narrator breaks in to announce: *When the days drew near for him to be taken up, he set his face to go to Jerusalem.* Again, as he is making his way to Jerusalem, Jesus says explicitly: "Yet today, tomorrow, and the next day I must be on my way, because it is impossible for a prophet to be killed outside of Jerusalem!"

It is, I have to admit, a bit heavy handed. But we get the point.

So in my mind's eye I begin on the top of the Mount of Olives, almost an hour's walk from my house, near a tiny cluster of houses in Bethpage on the road between Bethany and Jerusalem. I know the place intimately. Every Palm Sunday I hike up the mountain and watch the scene of Jesus' triumphant entry into Jerusalem played out in modern times, as it has been since early Christianity. A procession of hundreds passes on the main road, complete with scouts in uniforms, rivers of white-robed choir-boys, and marching bands. Children eager for applause lean out of their windows and call out: "Hosanna! Hosanna! Blessed is he who comes in the name of the Lord!"

I have always imagined Jesus passing that same path two thousand years ago, the crowds of bystanders throwing their cloaks on the ground to welcome him. Yet today I don't stop reading there. The sirens keep sounding outside of my window, making me uncomfortable, urging me on. For the first time I notice that Luke takes us away from that joy almost immediately. In the next sentence, he cuts to another, darker scene. As Jesus approaches the city, he stops and he weeps over Jerusalem. "If you, even you, had only recognized on this day the things that make for peace!" He laments, "But now they are hidden from your eyes. Indeed, the days will come upon you, when your enemies will set up ramparts around you and surround you, and hem you in on every side. They will crush you to the ground, you and your children within you."

It sends shivers. The beginning of the Palm Sunday march begins on the other side of the Mount of Olives, on the road from Jericho, where the sight of the city of Jerusalem is still completely obscured behind the mountain. Luke has executed the moment with film-like perfection. All is well—the spectators in the streets are celebrating. Jesus is riding his donkey amid the palms. He ascends the mountain slowly. Then, almost imperceptibly, he passes the ridge of the mountain, and out of nowhere the entire, ancient city of Jerusalem unfolds in front of his eyes.

And he weeps.

What does he see? Whatever the reason, for Luke, as with me—the Passion begins here, on the top of a mountain I know so well, a young man weeping not for his own life but for a city that seems bent, even two thousand years ago, on destroying itself.

What can I say? My curiosity has gotten the best of me. Joseph has awakened from his nap, and even though it is scorching outside I need to know what Jesus saw that afternoon at the beginning of his Passion. Why does it matter? Oddly, perhaps it is because the day on which I write this is Jerusalem Day, the day of the year in which the Israeli citizens of my city celebrate their capture of Jerusalem in the Six-Day War of 1967, and the day on which the Arab citizens mourn the city they lost. It is always a tense day, full of these conflicting emotions, and rumor in the streets is that there may be violence in the afternoon. I had been planning on staying inside. But Luke—why did he, alone among the four Gospel writers, add that scene on the Mount of Olives of Jesus weeping after his short, triumphal entry? What did he see?

I strap Joseph, clueless in his tiny striped sailor suit, into his stroller. Perhaps if we hurry, we'll make it back home again before any problems break out.

It is over a hundred degrees outside, as I make my way through the Damascus Gate into the Old City, turning down the Via Dolorosa, the road named after Jesus' Way of Suffering. At the end of the road I leave the city through the Lion's Gate and arrive at the foot of the Mount of Olives. By that time it is almost noon, and the sun is beating down on us. Joseph is asleep in his stroller as we ascend the mountain, and I smile at the thought of these unlikely journeys—Jesus on his donkey, me with my stroller. I have to walk slowly so that the weight of the stroller does not cause me to slide down the mountain and send my son careening into the valley below. By the time I arrive at the door of the monastery of Dominus Flevit—literally, "where God wept"—the entrance is shut.

"It's closed," the guard tells me. The idea of this—both symbolically and actually, after such a long journey—makes me want to collapse on the pavement and throw my hands up in despair. Yet I was raised to be polite, and I don't do things like throw my hands up in despair. Not in public, at least.

"Please," I beg him. "I walked all the way from Damascus Gate in the heat. With my baby."

"I can't," he insists.

A second guard comes to join us. "Come on," he chides the first guard. "What a shame—for her to walk all of this way in the heat. Give her a break."

The first guard seems to reconsider. He puts his finger over his lips and points. Now I see the problem—a group of ultra-extremist Jews have entered the compound, with two men with guns strapped over their shoulders standing behind them, standing watch. The guards are nervous, not sure what they are doing here. I too am not accustomed to seeing guns on holy ground.

We wait for them to leave, and then the guards bolt the door behind them.

"You have five minutes," the first one tells me.

It is enough. I wheel Joseph through the garden until I stop at the view extending in all directions in front of me: *Where Jesus wept*. I ask myself the question again: What did he see? Why did he weep?

The answer is that he saw everything. Luke, who is always paying such close attention both to story and to landscape, knows this very well. Jesus sees the entire story before it happens, just as I see it from my bench: The Temple in front of him, which he has already predicted will be destroyed, the Jewish inhabitants violently expelled from the city; the olive grove at the base of the mountain in Gethsemane, where one of his best friends will soon betray him; the stone walls of the Old City snaking along the mountainside, together with the gate leading to the way where he will carry his cross, where he has already predicted that he will suffer and be put to death; the Dome of the Church of the Holy Sepulcher, where he will be crucified, lies directly ahead. From this one space the entire story unfolds, waiting for him to step forward and enter into it. But first he stops. He looks. He sees it all.

This knowledge, I believe, is the real cross he carries for the rest of his Passion.

Two thousand years later I look out at the Old City from the same height. Joseph is beside me now, having awakened a few moments ago. He has just discovered his hands, and he is examining them in the light. A breeze is blowing over us, and for a moment everything seems so peaceful.

A single tear gathers in my eye, and I brush it away, here in this space just in front of the church, shaped in the form of a teardrop, because I know how the story ends. So did Luke.

The guard beckons. I say a quick prayer for the city I love—before he rushes me out the door.

Tuesday

Last night I walked with my husband and my son through the modern streets of downtown Jerusalem, where thousands of the most radical Jewish extremists had descended upon the city from surrounding settlements in the West Bank for Jerusalem Day. The streets were flooded with teenagers, high on their own adrenaline, chanting in unison and waving their flags with a zeal that scared me. I have learned to be afraid of them and wary of their message: that God's promise has been given to them and them alone, and that all non-Jews should leave the city. The Israeli shopkeepers around the square were equally nervous—just as my Arab neighbors, sure that trouble was brewing, had been tense all day. I kept Joseph close to me. Beside us a man who had come for the demonstrations also held the hand of his young son. A rifle was draped casually across his shoulder.

In the evening, when I returned home through the Old City, a young Arab boy stopped me from passing in the road.

"How much money do you want before I can cross?" I teased him in Arabic.

He blushed, realizing I was not his "enemy." "I'm sorry," he said. "I didn't let you pass because I thought that you were Jewish."

What am I to do with these words, spoken so casually, or with the young Orthodox Jewish girls, pictures of innocence with their long braids and beaming faces, who ask me on the end of my street if my road is safe to walk in because it is an Arab neighborhood? How do I reconcile the fact that I have awakened into the middle of my life to find myself living in a city I love and that I have chosen, but which is also a city full of anger and terrible violence on all sides? My life is not a film or a story like Luke's, with a discernable beginning, middle, and end. But if it were a film, or a Gospel for that matter, I would think: By the end of this story, surely someone will be dead.

Now it is Tuesday morning, and life has, miraculously, returned to normal. Joseph is once again down for his nap. But in Luke, Jesus is speaking of an apocalypse. They are his last teachings before his arrest, the prologue to all of the drama that will follow: the Temple will be destroyed and the world will turn to chaos. Jesus warns us:

> "Nation will rise against nation, and kingdom against kingdom; there will be great earthquakes, and in various places famines and plagues; and there will be dreadful portents and great signs from heaven. . . . When you see Jerusalem surrounded by armies, then know that its desolation has come near. Then those in Judea must flee to the mountains, and those inside the city must leave it, and those out in the country must not enter it; for these are the days of

vengeance, as a fulfillment of all that is written. Woe to those who are pregnant and to those who are nursing infants in those days!"

I put down my computer for a moment, and in a habit I can't break, I check on my son in his crib, to be sure he's still breathing.

In the afternoon, Joseph and I head to what's left of the Second Temple. During the life of Jesus it was in its final years, and we can assume that by the time Luke writes his story, everything is gone. I come here now because I can't help feeling that the destroyed Temple is the invisible character in the Gospel of Luke, casting its shadow over every line, especially in the last days of Jesus' life. As a reader that's what I imagine Jesus, who is deeply prophetic in Luke, saw most vividly from the top of that mountain: 70 CE, the first historical date I ever remember learning in my Catholic school. That the Temple's destruction is inevitable is what makes the story so haunting. What we readers know, and the characters of the Gospel don't, is that Jesus' Passion is also the story of the passion of a city, embodied in the life of a single man.

We make our way through the crowded main alley of the Old City, then through the metal detectors, until we reach the Western Wall plaza. I cross the plaza to the women's section, navigating my stroller into the river of prayers. The wall is so high that I have to crane my head to see the top, and above the top, the great blue sky. The wall is crowded today with Orthodox women, soldiers in their green uniforms, even a bride in her wedding dress, here to say one final prayer before the ceremony. Dozens of heads press against the grooved Herodian stones, the women lacing their hands among the thousands of slips of folded paper.

We can guess where Jesus actually walked in Jerusalem during his lifetime, but we know with certainty that he visited the Temple. Luke's Gospel, more than any other, insists on this. In Luke, Jesus is offered to the Temple in his infancy, and he preaches there as a precocious twelve year old. So we are not surprised that in Luke's Gospel, immediately after he weeps over Jerusalem, Jesus goes to the Temple, this time to drive out those selling their goods. "It is written," he says to them,

> "'My house shall be a house of prayer';
> but you have made it a den of robbers."

I wonder what he would have thought had he seen the rifles I just saw on the grounds of the church where he wept.

Only we, the readers, know that beneath this public fury is an invisible sorrow, for Jesus is like a son who can't stop yelling at his diabetic mother for sneaking off and buying candy that he knows is going to kill her in the end. The Temple is where Jesus spends every day of the last days of his life, preparing for his Passion by driving out the moneychangers, preaching to crowds, and presumably, praying like all these women around me. Luke tells us that the people "were spellbound by his words," while "the chief priests, the scribes, and the leaders of the people kept looking for a way to kill him."

It is hard now to appreciate how these Temple scenes must have read to early Christians, the haunting quality of Jesus walking through a place they know to be in ashes, in a city they know to be in ruins.

As for these things that you see, the days will come when not one stone will be left upon another; all will be thrown down.

I push through the crowds and place my folded piece of paper in the wall. Then I walk backward, pulling Joseph, until we exit, following the ancient local custom: We must never turn our backs on God.

Wednesday

All day long I've been searching for Jesus. Or is it Luke I'm searching for? I'm beginning to understand what Orthodox nuns and monks must feel like, living out the holy week in their monasteries, every Friday a Passion that they live in silence. I've been edgy all day, and as the week comes to its unavoidable conclusion, I've tried to hold fast to normal things—my husband, my child. I spend extra time making breakfast. I remember that Wednesday morning in the week of the Passion is the last good day.

I spend the afternoon with Joseph, searching for any remnants of the city that were here in Jesus' lifetime. The results are eerie. We descend a flight of stairs beneath Damascus Gate and find ourselves entering the ancient Roman gate, built not long after Jesus' death. The Roman stones on the ancient Cardo are massive squares of quarried stone, and I take off my shoes so that I can press against the coldness of them, can feel the grooves worn into them by carriage tracks. I press Joseph's little feet also, and we are transported back in time, closer to him, to a man of flesh and blood, who walked where we walk.

In the corner, scratched into the pavement, I find the remains of an ancient dice game Roman soldiers played. Later, we look through their garrison, made, archeologists believe, with the wide, beautiful stones of the destroyed Temple (for even now that Temple is an invisible character, casting its shadow over everything). Then we follow the ancient Roman Cardo all the way through the city, finally stopping to stare again at the Western Wall.

I feel particularly alone today—something about this searching makes me feel almost lost, looking for the ruins of someone else's life. And then I finally touch what is familiar about Jesus in the Passion. For most of Luke's Gospel, he is not a very likable character. He is difficult to please, a taskmaster, too quick to admonish everyone, his parents, and his disciples. "Let the dead bury their own dead," he tells a man who wishes to bury his father before following him. "Where is your faith?" he asks the disciples incredulously, when they are afraid that they might drown. In Luke's Gospel it seems that Jesus has followers, but he has no friends.

Yet I see a different, more vulnerable side to him in his last days in Jerusalem. He was not from here, but from the Galilee. His followers were fishermen, and he might have felt out of place during those last days in the city. Did he speak with a different accent than the men in the streets? Did his clothes give him away? Since the beginning of the story, when Mary and Joseph are sent from Nazareth to Bethlehem to give birth, there has been a sense in the Gospel that we must be strangers in the deepest moments of our destiny. I can't help feeling that in Luke's Gospel, the closer he comes to dying, the more human he becomes. He becomes a man capable of weeping.

Today the modern streets of the Old City are crowded with beggars, women from the countryside selling wild herbs, merchants, and children carried in their mother's arms. They remind me of what can be tender about Jesus. His world is peopled not just with Pharisees and men buying and selling in the Temple but with ordinary human beings. It is not the disciples, who are the buffoons of Luke's Gospel, toward whom Jesus is compassionate near the end of his life. It is the children who chase after Jesus in the Temple; the lepers and the blind who come to him to be healed; Zacchaeus, the tax collector, who climbs a tree to watch him passing on the road; the Roman centurion who sends his servant to be healed by him; the woman who anoints his feet with oil. Luke's world is crowded with dark villains, but also with small, anonymous saints, and it is these ordinary people who make Jesus not only God, but a man. They disarm him. They remind me of the man who sells falafel in front of my door, or the vendors I buy cheese from on the opposite side of town, or the children who play soccer against the walls of the Old City.

Today, Jesus' city is largely gone, destroyed less than half a century after his death by the Romans. So thorough was the destruction that I can hardly find anything left. Almost everything is from the century that followed.

People will faint from fear and foreboding of what is coming upon the world, for the powers of the heavens will be shaken.

I try not to think about the ordinary people who fled, the ground burning beneath their feet.

Thursday

And now the final Passion begins.

This morning, I awaken and make breakfast for my husband in bed, and we eat together from the same plate, which is my own approximation of what happens to Jesus in the text in the last supper. Sharing an intimate meal with those we most love, before heading to Gethsemane.

Part of what I find most heartbreaking about Luke's version of the last supper is its banality, despite every attempt by Jesus to make the event monumental. Only Jesus, the narrator, and we readers understand the gravity of the situation. The disciples are simply bit actors in a drama too big for them. They squabble among themselves, seemingly oblivious to the weight of what will follow. As when, an Iraqi friend of mine told me, his neighbors insisted on eating pastries and visiting cafes when they heard of the 2003 invasion, convinced that the world as they knew it could not be destroyed, so long as they kept drinking their coffee.

So here is Jesus, the Son of Man, at the last supper, telling his followers that he will soon suffer and enter the kingdom of God, as he has long predicted. And here are his disciples arguing, yet again, over who is the greatest among them. I imagine them fumbling over who will get the last pieces of bread. Peter, who will deny him, insists that he will never deny him. Among all of this mindless chattering is a man who is only a day away from being strung up on a mountaintop to die.

Luke has spent most of the Gospel trying to show us how divine Jesus is. But in this moment he is very much a man, completely and utterly alone. "I am among you as one who serves," he tells his disciples. "You are those who have stood by me in my trials." These words, it seems, are the closest he has come to confessing friendship. Yet the disciples are not his friends, or perhaps they are just his very imperfect friends, which in the end is better than dying alone. They will not stand by him in the trials that follow.

Now I wheel Joseph into Gethsemane on the Mount of Olives. It is early morning, the quietest I've ever seen it here. Birds are singing in the ancient, gnarled branches of the olive trees. Beside them, in the garden, pink flowers blossom against a background of blue sky and the snaking walls of the Old City.

I open Luke and read. *He came out and went, as was his custom, to the Mount of Olives; and the disciples followed him.* The mountain is also a character in Luke's Gospel. Earlier in the Gospel he mentions that, while Jesus preached in the Temple during the day, he returned to the mountain to sleep at night. It is here that he wept over the city. It is here that he comes to pray. Now, it is here that he comes to beg his father for release. Luke's God is interior, discovered not in the Temple but in silence. This is why, perhaps, Jesus does not just leave the disciples alone, as he does in the other Gospels. *Then he withdrew from them,* Luke says. It is a pattern we have come to recognize, for Luke's Jesus has a habit of going off on his own. He withdraws into the quietness of his own heart to prepare himself for what he must do.

Now, it is time. Soon Judas will come with the soldiers to arrest him. So an angel comes to strengthen Jesus. Oh, Luke's angels! Appearing since the beginning of the story: to Zechariah, to Mary, to the shepherds, and now finally to Jesus, kneeling on the mountain, praying until "his sweat became like great drops of blood falling down on the ground." I can see her, almost, with her calm hand, her translucent wings. Jesus collapsed on the stone in anguish, the angel leaning over him.

"Father, if you are willing, remove this cup from me; yet, not my will but yours be done."

When Jesus returns to the disciples, he finds them "sleeping because of grief," Luke says.

"Why are you sleeping?" he asks them. "Get up and pray that you may not come into the time of trial."

I peer inside Joseph's stroller. He has also fallen asleep, with his hands half closed, just beside his face. I lower a cloth over the front to protect him from the sun. We have a long journey ahead of us still.

Sleep, my love, I think. Sleep while you can.

Before the betrayal takes place, let me explain what I find most painful about this city. It is the intimacy of the enemies. I can never get used to it—and rarely a day goes by when this singular fact does not break my heart. In Jerusalem, my neighbors are friends until they are enemies. The Arab and the Israeli sit in cafes together. They walk through the Old City together. They speak a few words of one another's languages.

The Israeli soldier stops in an Arab snack shop to purchase falafel. The Palestinian girl practices her Hebrew homework between her work shifts at a nearby hotel.

Yesterday, a man spoke to me about Joseph in Hebrew and then took him in his arms. I responded to him with a few sentences of faulty Hebrew, and we smiled at one another. We connected. It was only later, when I met him again, that I realized that I had been mistaken about who he was. The man was an Arab who assumed that I was Jewish and so spoke to me in what he thought was my own language.

An intimacy of enemies. Any conflict is sad, but a conflict among friends is heartbreaking.

Here we go. Judas approaches. He kisses Jesus. "Judas, is it with a kiss that you are betraying the Son of Man?"

One of the disciples, seeing what is going to happen, strikes the slave of the high priest, cutting off his ear. Then Jesus calls out a plea, for me the hardest sentence of the entire Gospel, before reaching out to heal the wounded man:

"No more of this!"

Friday

Today I set out early, strapping Joseph to my body with a carrier, knowing all of the flights of stairs and sudden turns on the Via Dolorosa that make using a stroller impossible. Today I want him close to me.

Is there something morbid about bringing my son on this journey? In Arabic, the word for being pregnant is *haml,* which literally means "to carry." "I'm carrying" is what I told people to express the strange phenomena of carrying a child in my womb, of creating a life inside me. I remember that now, understanding that Luke's Gospel is framed by these two realities—carrying a child and this same child carrying a cross.

A sword will pierce your own soul too.

The city is just opening. Old men are sweeping the area in front of their shops, setting out cartons of plums and peaches. Women are unloading their bags of grape leaves and sage onto the cobblestones to sell. A truck carries heavy wooden crosses to the Lion's Gate, where pilgrims will drag them throughout the day down the Way of the Cross. We make our way to the first station, where Jesus is condemned to death, and stand silently in the middle of the crowded street. Then we descend beneath the arch called Ecce Homo, *Behold the Man*, and into the earth to the lithostrotos, an immense Roman-era chamber beneath the ground.

It is freezing. The floor is covered with giant Roman stones from the streets of the second century. The chamber is completely empty except for the two of us; more games from Roman soldiers are etched into the ground. I think of the Roman guards in Luke, mocking and beating Jesus, blindfolding him and demanding: "Prophesy! Who is it that struck you?" They suddenly become real to me, not only because of the Roman games on the ground, but because of the real soldiers I passed this morning leaning against the wall and chatting on their cell phones, not so much villains, as we are tempted to portray them, but bored teenagers trying to pass the time.

Tradition names this as the place where Jesus was condemned to death. In Luke's version of the story the crowd accuses Jesus of incitement, stirring up people all over the country with his teachings. Pilate asks him if he is a Galilean.

An outsider. Not of this place. A stranger, sent to the city to die.

Pilate sends him off to Herod, who has wanted him to die for some time now. Yet even Herod lets him go free. He mocks him, and his soldiers dress him in elegant robes, like the fool in Shakespeare's plays who we recognize as the only sane character in the entire drama. Then he sends him back to Pilate, who desires to flog and release him, but a crowd consisting of the "chief priests, the leaders, and the people" insists that he crucify him.

"Crucify, crucify him!"

"Why? What evil has he done?"

But they kept urgently demanding with loud shouts that he should be crucified; and their voices prevailed. Jesus is not condemned to death by Pilate or Herod in Luke. An angry mob puts him to death, and in exchange Pilate lets Barabbas, a true killer, go free.

If we can look at this as literature, then the moment is an indictment against a society gone mad. The exchange of an innocent man with a guilty one is just one example of how far the world Jesus inhabits has fallen, how lost and morally bankrupt it has become. Yet it says something about the moral complexity of Luke's world that Pilate, who wishes to let Jesus go, is the one who must do the dirty work of finally sentencing him to death. Just as in the wings, Peter, Luke's beloved disciple, is right now betraying his best friend. Even Judas falls only because "Satan entered" him. Luke's world is full of bad men, but the cruelest tasks of his Gospel require the kindest men to carry them out.

Joseph is already hungry, and we have only made it through two stations. But we are alone in the prison chamber, and so I take him out of his carrier, pull him up against me, and in that room under the earth where Pilate condemns Jesus to death, I nurse my son.

When we have finished, we enter the streets again. The sun is already beating down on us. For the rest of the journey we will not so much live Luke's Passion as meditate on all that goes missing. For almost all of the traditional stations are gone in his account. Luke's Passion is spare, void of much of the agony of the other Gospels, but also missing many of the consolations. So that when Joseph and I arrive at the end of the street, where tradition says that Jesus falls for the first time, I can hold my child against me. No, not in Luke, I think. No, he simply keeps walking.

But then my heart cries out a few steps down, where the tradition holds that Jesus met his mother. For that encounter also is missing in Luke—a look of recognition between a mother and her son that I am just beginning to understand. I need that look. I need it not for Jesus, but for Mary, who deserves to be more than a narrative tool in Luke's story. She is a real human being who surely longs to touch her son one last time. Luke, you have sent us angels—but where are the humans in the time of need?

We keep walking, Joseph looking out at the streets in bewilderment.

Today the market is crowded with boys selling socks and alarm clocks and old men shouting out at passing tourists. I wonder if this approximates the public spectacle that must have accompanied Jesus' Passion. How odd it feels to think of death mixed in so easily with spices and syrupy desserts for sale! Next we arrive at a corner I have walked past a hundred times. This time I stop in the chapel to pray, for this corner is a rare station included in Luke's account: *Simon of Cyrene helps Jesus carry his cross.* In Luke's version of the story, Simon is seized from the crowd. I have never understood this station. Why would the soldiers make a passerby carry the cross? Why would they desire to relieve the suffering of Jesus even for a moment? I can't make any sense of it, and for that reason alone it feels real to me, part of the actual events, for real life never fits into a neat scheme of what is plausible. Real life simply happens, with all of its strangeness and contradictions, a man walking down the street, possibly on his way to a meeting or to drink a cup of coffee, suddenly roped into the central moment in salvation history.

We are nearing the end of the journey. In a small alley I pass the space where in Luke, and in Luke alone, Jesus lives out one bizarre and terrible moment in the Passion before he is led to die. He will not have his face wiped clean by Veronica. Nor will he fall a second or third time. In Luke, a group of women follow after Jesus, beating their breasts and wailing for him. And Jesus turns to them and says:

> "Daughters of Jerusalem, do not weep for me, but weep for yourselves and for your children. For the days are surely coming when they will say: 'Blessed are the barren, and the wombs that never bore, and the breasts that never nursed.' Then they will begin to say to the mountains, 'Fall on us';

and to the hills, 'Cover us.' For if they do this when the
wood is green, what will happen when it is dry?"

It feels, for a moment, that the words are directed at me. But I
do not do what I want to do. I do not collapse in the middle of
the road or on a flight of stairs busy with passersby, and hold my
son against my chest. I do not cry for the market in West Jerusalem I shop in every week that has been bombed or the pizza
place bombed or the church in Bethlehem attacked with tank
fire. I do not cry for the hospital where my son was born, whose
Virgin Mary statue was peppered with bullet holes. I do not cry
for the two oblivious Palestinian boys attacked and stabbed by a
mob of eighty Israeli teenage boys while shopping last month in
the Jerusalem mall, or the eight Jewish boys in a yeshiva gunned
down by a Palestinian man here in March, or the checkpoints,
or the security guards at the door of every Israeli café. I do not
cry because I have chosen this life. Joseph is kicking, clearly
uncomfortable. The sun is getting hotter. We must keep moving.

At the end of the morning we climb a set of stairs leading
from the market, make our way through a winding street on
the rooftops, and finally descend into the Church of the Holy
Sepulcher from above. I am exhausted from walking, from carrying my son, from living Luke's Passion all week long. Near
the enormous front door of the church I climb a flight of stone
stairs to the Chapel of the Crucifixion, where a mosaic of Jesus
crucified stands against hundreds of candles and the imprint of
millions and millions of prayers. Red lanterns sway from the
ceiling. The air is heavy with incense. A Greek Orthodox priest
in a long black robe eyes us warily from behind his long beard. I
find a place to sit on the cool marble benches built into the wall,
and I pull out my Gospel of Luke one final time:

Jesus turns to those who have crucified him. And he prays to God: "Father, forgive them; for they do not know what they are doing."

A sign is hung above him: *This is the King of the Jews.*

One of the criminals beside him taunts: "Are you not the Messiah? Save yourself and us!" But the other criminal begs: "Jesus, remember me when you come into your kingdom." And Jesus replies: "Truly I tell you, today you will be with me in Paradise."

Darkness comes over the land. The curtain of the Temple is torn in two. And Jesus cries out in a loud voice: "Father, into your hands I commend my Spirit." When he has said this, he breathes his last.

Joseph, very suddenly, has fallen asleep against me. I take him out of his carrier, and I press his face against my face. The stones of the bench are cool against us. We sit together in the Chapel of the Crucifixion, with his arms around my neck, and both of us rest.

Sunday

"Father, into your hands I commend my Spirit."

In the midst of all of this, Jesus makes an oblation of himself. He offers himself up to God. It does not erase the other moments. But it makes them bearable. It is as though he is whispering, quietly: *Yes, it is as terrible as you have heard. But salvation is here, in this moment.*

Once upon a terrible time, a child is born.

It allows me to keep going long enough for Jesus to be well again, to rise up three days later. Long enough for Luke to continue not only his Gospel but the Book of Acts—for us to know that it is not all in vain—that in the midst of the fallen world a frail church will be built by equally frail men, and yet it will last. It will last, even until now. Even here. For in the end, Luke's Gospel will always be the Gospel of birth, of life being born in the ruins.

These days I read the Bible in Arabic, which means I read from right to left, from end to beginning. I turn the pages backward, so that the Passion is situated at the front of the story, where the birth story is supposed to begin. It makes sense to me. As T. S. Eliot put it, "The end is where we start from."

So let me, too, end with my beginning. It is early spring of 2007, and in the street in front of my house in Jerusalem, in a moment of extreme violence, several hundred men do not cry out but instead fall down on their knees and pray, and offer themselves to God.

I go inside, and my husband looks up from his newspaper. "I want to have a child," I tell him.

For in the end—these two carryings—that of a child and of a cross, become one. Life comes into suffering—and in Luke's version of the story, life is always triumphant.

My husband and I will always believe that we conceived our child on the Feast of Good Friday. Who knows if we are right?

All we do know is that he was born near Christmas Day, in a town called Bethlehem.

4

Reading John's Passion

Narrative in the Fourth Gospel

JAY PARINI

I begin my reading of John with a brief note of autobiography. My father was a Baptist minister, and for the last fifty years of his life (give or take) he carried a small copy of the Gospel of John in his jacket pocket. It was almost talismanic. He read it over and over, and he often read it aloud at the breakfast table, always in the King James translation. From those times, the harmonies, beauties, and occasional discordances of this Gospel have lodged in my head, in my heart, in places where they cannot be taken away from me. Thus, it was with some trepidation that I recently sat down to reread the Gospel afresh, wondering how it would sound if read simply as a narrative, as literature.

Some years ago I had made an effort to study the Gospels in the light of modern biblical scholarship, thinking about the various sources, looking at the puzzling manuscript traditions. To one brought up in the traditions of the Baptist Church, as I was, the scholarship (much of it based on the ground-breaking work of nineteenth-century German scholars, as summarized by Albert Schweitzer's *The Quest of the Historical Jesus*) came as a genuine and troubling revelation. The Gospels were hardly the straight-forward retelling of the Jesus story as I had imagined. They were problematic texts, written long after the time of Jesus, perhaps composite voices gathered and fashioned with fictional intention: shaping and reshaping the stories that didn't sit easily cheek by jowl; that is, each evangelist worked from unique sources, although at least the Synoptic Gospels had a common source as well. John, as I hadn't quite realized, stood out as something very different from the others.

Biblical scholars, of course, ask many good questions about John and its unique character: Who wrote the Fourth Gospel? When was it written—and for whom? What were the author's sources? And why is it so different from the other Gospels? The author of this Gospel was almost certainly *not* the disciple who walked with Jesus and was beloved of him (a rival with Peter for the affections of the Lord). Might he have been a Hellenistic convert to Christianity who wrote somewhere at the end of the first century or the beginning of the second century? J. A. T. Robinson has argued that this Gospel might actually be much earlier, perhaps even before the destruction of the Second Temple in 70 CE, although this is a minority opinion. Did the writer know the other Gospels or have access to Gospels or Gospel traditions that we don't even know about?

The only sure thing is that the Gospel of John is different; that it stands alone, seeming to have little in common with its cousins, Matthew, Mark, and Luke (the so-called Synoptic Gospels); and that the difference has a lot to do with its mode of narration. So while there was some trepidation in my looking at the Gospel of

John as literature, it also seemed very natural, for I've spent my life thinking about, and often writing, stories. I have also written several biographies, finding biography one of the most difficult genres because of the choices I have to make regarding what to include, what to leave out, and how to arrange the material to reveal something about the inner identity of the person I am writing about. And whatever else we might say about the Gospel of John, it is clearly a story, indeed, one of the primary stories of Western civilization—and one of the world's most challenging biographies.

John—whoever he was—was a good writer, often poetic and inherently theological (even philosophical). He knew very well the task at hand: to present the life and teachings of Jesus in a way that would persuade an audience of their importance and meaning—an audience at the convergence of the Jewish and Gentile worlds. The Jesus who emerges in the Fourth Gospel is bold, singular, and very unlike his counterpart in the Synoptic Gospels. He doesn't speak in the short, pithy parables and aphorisms of Matthew, Mark, and Luke, but in an overtly didactic, if sometimes enigmatic, fashion, using metaphors and other figures of speech. Many of them appear in a vivid series of "I am" statements that Jesus makes in reference to himself, such as, *I am* the good shepherd; *I am* the bread, *I am* the light, *I am* in the Father, *I am* in you. Frequently, Jesus expands on them in deliberate teaching, as when he gives his last instructions to his disciples in chapters 14 and 15. He says to them, "I am the vine, you are the branches." This seems to be laying the groundwork for a church, but not explicitly. This is not a parable but a metaphor. And strikingly, while some of the language here refers to lopping off branches that do not bear fruit and casting them into the fire to be burned (which sounds a lot like the apocalyptic preaching of John the Baptist in Matthew and Luke), the Fourth Gospel emphasizes the close relationship between Jesus the vine and his disciples the branches, suggesting something like a permanent connection between them. Developing the metaphor, John has Jesus say, "Those who abide in me and I in them bear much fruit." He extends the metaphor even further when he instructs them to "abide in my love" and calling the disciples "friends." Then, in one of the many ways we will see John folding the Passion into such metaphors and discourses throughout his Gospel, Jesus says to the branches/disciples/friends, "No one has greater love than this, to lay down one's life for one's friends." And, of course, this is just what Jesus is about to do, to lay down his life for his friends—literally.

To get at John's point here, I think of the way he treats one of my favorite moments in any of the Gospels, recounted in Luke 17:20–21:

> Once Jesus was asked by the Pharisees when the kingdom of God was coming, and he answered, "The kingdom of God is not coming with things that can be observed; nor will they say, 'Look, here it is!' or 'There it is!' For, in fact, the kingdom of God is among you."

I remember it best, however, in the King James Version my father read: "The kingdom of God is within you."

John runs with this same idea, returning to it again and again. In the Passion Narrative it appears when Jesus says to Pilate: "My kingdom is not from this world." But it is also present in the opening verses of John:

> In the beginning was the Word, and the Word was with God, and the Word was God. He was in the beginning with

God. All things came into being through him, and without him not one thing came into being. What has come into being in him was life, and the life was the light of all people. The light shines in the darkness, and the darkness did not overcome it.

That is, Jesus in John lives outside of time; he is eternal from the start; he may be lord of a kingdom, but it is not an earthly kingdom. This makes John the most mystical of the Gospels. The Cosmic Christ emerges here, a figure without a beginning or an end, a character somehow related to but nevertheless detached from the person of Jesus of Nazareth, who must carry the heavy weight of this larger mythic presence. From the outset, he is "the Word" who existed before time. This is a far cry from the helpless baby in the manger in Bethlehem, a child who sleeps in the barn with animals, with shepherds outside keeping watch over their flocks. (Only in Matthew and Luke do we get the Christmas story at all, and these stories are shockingly different, difficult to harmonize.) In John, Jesus becomes, weirdly, something like the divine spark of the Gnostics, identified with light itself.

In the Gnostic tradition the universe was summoned into being by an evil god, or demiurge, who created a dark world. In this universe one looks for mystic insight, a divine spark, something to illumine the world and repair the brokenness—as in the Kabbalistic idea of *tikkun olam*, which means, "to repair the world." Various Gnostic ideas had arisen in the last decade of the first century, and many of these ideas had immense appeal to early Christians. John gestures in their direction here, which suggests that he had them in mind as part of his audience. He also appeals to the Hellenistic reader who had some knowledge of the traditions behind the word *logos*. As we know, the apostle

Paul and other early Christian were drawn to the ideas of Philo of Alexandria, who adapted the Greek notion of *logos* from Aristotle and, before him, Heraclitus, who saw the reasoning power of the human mind as a governing principle in the universe. It is hard to understand what any of these writers and thinkers meant by *logos*, but it certainly had some relation to the reasoning mind and to the idea of the word itself; there has always been something purposefully ambiguous about the "Word."

In the Platonic world the material and spiritual worlds had an independent existence. To some extent the Stoics rejected this idea and leaped on the word *logos* as a mediating term between spirit and matter. Philo, who lived at the time of Jesus, seized on the term as he attempted a synthesis of Jewish and Greek thought, a synthesis that appealed to Hellenistic Christians, such as the writer of John's Gospel. (The Epistle to the Hebrews has similar notions.) One can see the development of the idea of *logos* from the early Greeks, where it stands for "reason," to the Stoics, who made reason itself into a kind of god. As a Jew, Philo could hardly tolerate having reason as God; God was God. And so the idea of *logos* morphed into a secondary but divine principle, as Philo took full possession of the *logos* in its double meaning as "word" and "reason."

In his Gospel, John opens with his prologue of eighteen verses, which, as noted above, substitutes for the miraculous birth in Matthew and Luke. Jesus is not simply the Christ; he is more. He is *logos*, an eternal principle. He is therefore indestructible. He exists before the world and after it. He combines the spirit world and matter in a unique way, and those who understand him, who accept the divine logic of the *logos*, as it were, are "saved," as Christians often say. The saving grace alluded to here is the knowledge of time as a continuous loop, a mystical king-dom that cannot be seen, or described, or counted, or clocked.

At the same time, in a remarkable way, John tells us, "the Word became flesh and lived among us . . . full of grace and truth."This, too, comes through in the Passion of John's Gospel, when we read it—as one must read, I argue—without recourse to history or literal truth. The Passion in John is a riveting and distinct narrative, working hard to create a *mythos*—a story with symbolic import that blazes in the reader's memory. For in the Passion, the Word that became flesh dies.

Such a story means that whoever wrote this Gospel was not bound by the actual events of Jesus' life; rather, this Gospel is a stylized narrative that reads like well-crafted fiction, with a care-ful layering of stories and slow building up of events. The result is a very different story about Jesus, one that gives us scenes not found in the other Gospels, including, for example, the wedding at Cana, the story of the Samaritan woman at the well, the raising of Lazarus from the dead, the healing of the sick man at Bethesda, the washing of the disciples' feet, and so forth. There is also a wealth of new material in the form of sayings and discourses that are quite different in form and content. And there is John's reworking of early traditions.

Throughout the Fourth Gospel the author remains a writer at heart, like a fiction writer who offers luminous and precise details, giving exact names to minor figures in the story, as in chapter 18, where he refers to the servant who lost his ear in a skirmish with Peter as Malchus. It is the exact naming of the servant here that catches and holds our attention. It makes us think, *This writer knows his stuff*. And there is a great deal of local knowledge in this Gospel, too, suggesting that the author either knew Palestine well or wanted to give the impression that he did. Often, scenes are set in specific places and with great detail—the way novelists and poets work. In chapter 5 John sets the scene for the healing of a man who had been ill for thirty-eight years with GPS-like precision: "In Jerusalem by the Sheep Gate there is a pool, called in Hebrew Beth-zatha, which has five porticos." It is as if John is inviting his readers to go and see. In chapter 6 John makes reference to "the place where they had eaten the bread after the Lord had given thanks," which sounds a lot like a stop on a sightseeing tour—an early reference to pilgrimage?

An even more striking bit of detail appears earlier in that chapter when John, alone among the Gospels, notes that the feeding of the five thousand occurred when "Passover, the festival of the Jews, was near." With this detail he links the story of the five thousand to Jesus' declaration that he is the "bread of life" later in the chapter and to the breaking of bread and giving thanks at the last supper in the Synoptic Gospels. Such exactness is the sign of a real writer, one who understands the use of place and time, and one who uses them to assert credibility and give the narrative a circumstantial grounding—and frequently to point to meaning beyond the narrative itself.

In John's Passion Narrative such details dramatically and substantively affect the story, as when (very unlike his counterparts) he places the crucifixion on the day *before* Passover, at the time when the Passover lambs were being slain. To drive this point home, John adds to the Passion Narrative in the Synoptic Gospels a story about the Jewish leaders' asking that the legs of the crucified be broken so that they will die faster and their bodies can be taken down from the crosses before Sabbath/Passover begins. To comply with the request, the soldiers proceed to break the legs of the crucified men—only to find that Jesus is already dead. They don't need to break his legs. Thus, in one of John's many references to Jewish scriptures, he shows that Jesus, like a Passover lamb, is without blemish. If we have been reading carefully, however, we know that something like this had to have happened, for in John's Gospel—and only in John's Gospel— John the Baptist identifies Jesus as "the Lamb of God who takes away the sin of the world" *at the very beginning of the story* (1:29)!

By showing how Jesus' death is the death of a Passover lamb, however, John has to give up the notion that the last supper is a Passover meal, as it is in the Synoptic Gospels. But since John has already used the bread of the last supper in chapter 6 (as we have seen), he can introduce another story—Jesus' washing the disciples' feet—and he does it to great effect, since it resonates with Mary's anointing of Jesus' feet, Jesus' laying down his life for his friends, and the commandment to "love one another [just] as I have loved you."

Yet another foreshadowing of the Passion appears early in John's narrative, one that he borrows from the Jesus traditions appearing in the Synoptic Gospels—the cleansing of the Temple. But while Matthew, Mark, and Luke put this story at the end of Jesus' public ministry (just before he is arrested and the Passion begins), John puts it at the beginning, again making the Passion part of the whole story. What's more, he not only *moves* the story but also *adds* to it in a way that reflects the double meaning that is so typical of his narrative style. In chapter 2 John has Jesus say what Matthew and Mark treat as a false accusation in the trial narratives: "Destroy this temple, and in three days I will raise it up." Freud has noted that all dreams of a house are dreams of the individual soul. Thus, in a sense, John anticipates Freud in this passage, for when Jesus' accusers take him literally, he explains to his readers that Jesus was referring to his body and foreshadows the three days between his death and the raising of his body, or, we might say, the transforming of his body into spirit. (Note the way John also double-speaks when he refers to Jesus' crucifixion as being "lifted up" in 3:14; 8:28; and 12:32, 34). Yet one more point about the way John uses the story of the cleansing of the Temple is that he concludes it by adding that it is only *after* the resurrection that Jesus' disciples understood the meaning of the saying—"After he was raised from the dead, his disciples remembered that he had said this"—perhaps showing how the Spirit will guide their understanding of what Jesus said and did.

In fact, Jesus worries a good deal about the fate of his disciples. What will become of them? It was always a key idea among the early Christians that Jesus would return one day. But John transmogrifies this notion. Jesus, as Christ, was here before us, and he will remain here, even after the physical Jesus has departed. John 14:18–19 may hold the key to this Gospel: "I will not leave you orphaned; I am coming to you. In a little while the world will no longer see me, but you will see me; because I live, you also will live." That is to say, this temporal business will soon end. My enemies will get me, and I will die. But I can outleap the limits of place and time. I'm not bound to those rules. The parameters of worldly time don't apply. If you're in accord with my teachings, and if you understand them properly, you also are free of the restraints of place and time.

John makes this clear in chapter 11 in Jesus' conversation with Martha just before raising her brother Lazarus. When she chides Jesus for not being there when her brother needed him, he responds, "Your brother will rise again." Then, in a remarkable response to her profession of faith in Lazarus's rising again "in the resurrection on the last day," Jesus reveals himself to her in the words Christians commonly use in funerals, "I am the resurrection and the life. Those who believe in me, even though they die, will live, and everyone who lives and believes in me will never die." The story of the raising of Lazarus is amazingly told. The most familiar part of the story is Martha's response to Jesus' command to take away the stone sealing Lazarus's tomb, marvelously rendered in the King James Version as, "Lord, by this time he stinketh." Jesus chides her, reminding her that if she believed, she would see the glory of God. Then after praying he calls Lazarus to come out. And he does—with his hands and feet bound and his face wrapped in a cloth. But what happened after they unbound him and let him go? He shows up in chapter 12 at a dinner that he and his sisters give for Jesus—sitting at the table, we are told. One wonders about the conversation! Did anyone ask him what had happened—what he saw? If they did, John shows no interest in reporting it, apparently thinking other things were more important. And to make his point, John—ever the writer—continues his account of the dinner by rewriting stories found in Matthew, Mark, and Luke.

First, he tells us Martha served the meal, much as she did at another dinner recounted by Luke (10:38–42). But more striking, he puts the anointing of Jesus at this dinner (rather than at the house of Simon the Leper as in Matthew 26:6 and Mark 14:3) and identifies the woman who anoints Jesus as Lazarus's sister Mary. As in Mark, she uses "pure nard" worth three hundred denarii, which Judas complains is a waste of good money. Jesus scolds him, however, saying: "Leave her alone. She bought it so that she might keep it for the day of my burial. You always have the poor with you, but you do not always have me." This is an astonishing statement in that Jesus explicitly warns his disciples and friends that he will not be around much longer. This narrative turn is unique to John, although the phrasing about the poor being always "with you" refers back to Deuteronomy 15:11, one of the countless inter-textual links with the Hebrew scriptures that give the Gospels a sense of inevitability and scriptural fulfillment. In preaching to a Jewish community, it was no doubt essential that John refer frequently to its sacred texts.

But John's attention to the Jews in this story goes beyond references to their scriptures. In fact, and this is the other important thing in the story of the raising of Lazarus, the Jews are a part of the story from beginning to end. We see them consoling Martha, following Mary, weeping with Mary, noting how much Jesus loves Lazarus—though some of them, like Mary earlier in the story, wondered if Jesus could not have done more if he had arrived earlier. But most important of all, many of the Jews believed in Jesus when they saw what he had done. The same themes show up in chapter 8, when the Jews who believed in Jesus were first confused and then angered when Jesus tells them they will be free if they "continue in my word." "If you were Abraham's children, you would be doing what Abraham did, but now you are trying to kill me, a man who has told you the truth that I heard from God. This is not what Abraham did." The passage builds to the climax: "Very truly, I tell you, whoever keeps my word will never see death." This sets up the resurrection in interesting ways.

The chapter ends with an enigmatic assertion: "Before Abraham was, I am." This is yet another of the many "I am" statements. This one is particularly memorable, as it is a grammatical impossibility, at least in human terms. The syntax dislocates the reader from time as *chronos*, or linear time, into time as *durée* (to adopt a term from Henri Bergson) or circular, eternal time. Such stories should give us pause when thinking about the role of "the

Jews" in the Fourth Gospel. It appears to be more complex than a quick reading would suggest.

The final outcome to the story of the raising of Lazarus makes clear what John has in mind when he refers to "the Jews" as the bad guys: "the chief priests and the Pharisees" who call a meeting and plan to put Jesus to death when they hear that many of their compatriots believe in him. And John makes this identification at precisely the moment when Caiaphas, the high priest, declares that it is better to have one man die for the people than to have the whole nation destroyed. Even if he says the high priest said this without knowing the real meaning of his words, John certainly believes it to be true, for it fits perfectly with his claim that Jesus is the Lamb of God who takes away the sin of the world.

It is also consistent with John's irony that the raising of Lazarus, the last of Jesus' signs in John, is the one that seals Jesus' fate. And it is fitting that Mary's anointing of Jesus at the dinner given for him in recognition of what he has done is the first scene in the final act of John's Passion.

Before looking at this final act, however, one more word about John and "the Jews." In the crazy, mixed-up world of Roman Judea, all kinds of things could happen. John treats the high priest's words in 11:50 as ironic—as a writer might. What the high priest says in John's Gospel could also be taken at face value. After all, it would not be surprising if Jewish leaders negotiated hard with their Roman overlords and took part in power plays when occasion afforded an opening. Such things happen in brutal regimes. That said, whatever role the leaders of the Temple may have played in the crucifixion of Jesus, it does not justify the persecution, pogroms, and discrimination that Jews have had to endure at the hands of Christians—not to mention the atrocities of the

Holocaust. To claim otherwise is not only to miss the complexity of John's treatment of the Jews but also to reject its message.

"The hour has come for the Son of Man to be glorified," Jesus declares to Andrew and Philip when those who had gathered in Jerusalem for the Passover came to them wishing to see Jesus (chapter 12). The words are poignant, setting the stage for the remainder of the drama, the crucifixion of the Word made flesh, here ironically described as Jesus' "glorification." Earlier in John's Gospel, Jesus had spoken of the "hour" more obliquely. He first used the term when changing the water into wine. Jesus says to his mother, "My hour has not yet come." The time of the Christ is timeless, of course; but it will take the release of Jesus from time, in the crucifixion, to establish him outside of time and place. Mary wants Jesus to do something, it seems: to perform a miracle. These miracles are out of the space-time continuum, and Jesus seems annoyed by her demands. He hesitates. Yet he decides to begin performing signs, which lifts him above time and place. Even so, his repeated refrain is "the hour is *coming*," only rarely saying, as he does to the woman at the well, that it impinges on the present. Only now, at the end, has the hour come.

The Passion itself begins in the garden, a place that Jesus and his disciples obviously knew. They often met there, perhaps, and so Judas knew where to lead the soldiers, although there is nothing in John about Judas kissing Jesus to reveal him. Indeed, in the Fourth Gospel it is not obvious that Judas has any defining role in turning Jesus over to the authorities. He is simply carrying out a role that was assigned to him. Nor is this the only difference in the way John develops the scene in the garden. In the Gospel of Mark Jesus, is deeply distressed in the garden, throwing himself down on the ground as he prays—three times—that he not have to die. Luke softens the story: Jesus *kneels* and prays only once that the cup might be removed. Strikingly, John omits Jesus' prayer completely, going straight to the arrest. But this should not surprise us, given John's exalted portrayal of Jesus. How could he have Jesus ask that he not have to die, even if in the other Gospels he finally strengthens his resolve and commits to doing God's will? John, in fact, had already dealt with this question much earlier in his Gospel, apparently having in mind the tradition found in the Synoptic Gospels. In chapter 12, when he first uses the phrase "the hour has come for the Son of man to be glorified," he has Jesus tell Andrew and Philip, "Now my soul is troubled. And what should I say—'Father, save me from this hour'? No, it is for this reason that I have come to this hour." How can we read these words without thinking of Jesus' prayer in the Synoptic Gospels? And how can we think other than that John completely rejects the notion that Jesus could consider trying to avoid what he was sent to do? Indeed, in John's version of the garden scene, Jesus seems almost eager to get the process going and to assume his sacrificial role.

The opening verses of chapter 18 are quite tense, as a narrative, as the confrontation between Jesus and the soldiers leads to the scuffle where Peter draws his sword and cuts off the right ear of the high priest's slave, Malchus. The drama unfolds at perfect speed, with concentrated force, although John the theologian can never quite rest, and Jesus even in the midst of his trauma always seems defiantly cosmic: "I am he," he repeats, in such a way that the soldiers fall to the ground. It's almost as if God spoke from the clouds. And he tells Peter to put his sword back, saying, "Am I not to drink the cup that the Father has given me?" The theology of drinking keeps flowing; the water of life passes from mouth to mouth. It flows from the baptism of Jesus at the outset through the woman at the well to this moment in the garden.

The narrative drum beats now. Arrested, Jesus is hauled off before Annas, the father-in-law of a high priest—again, this is material unique to John. Then comes the interrogation by Pilate, who asks Jesus directly if he is the king of the Jews. The response of Jesus to his question is better in Mark's Gospel, where he says: "If you say so." That seems, to me, more like Jesus, a sly responder who delights in ambiguity. In John, Jesus grows theological in response to a simple question: "You say that I am a king. For this I was born, and for this I came into the world, to testify to the truth. Everyone who belongs to the truth listens to my voice." Obviously annoyed by such a response, Pilate asks: "What is truth?"

We don't get to hear what Jesus replies, unfortunately, but he would have had something to say. The narrative leaps quickly to Pilate saying: "I find no case against him." But the Jewish torment-ers insist that Jesus has committed the sin of elevating himself above God, and Pilate finally gives in. Jesus is taken away to be crucified and forced to carry his own cross to Golgotha, "The Place of the Skull"—no reference to Simon of Cyrene here. In John, Jesus does not need anyone to carry his cross.

The actual crucifixion is described succinctly in the Fourth Gospel. John does not belabor any point, nor does he trouble to milk the scene for all its emotional content. The agony of Jesus doesn't keep his focus. Interestingly, John places Mary the mother of Jesus, along with others, such as Mary Magdalene, at the site of the cross. In chapter 19 there is a flicker of a scene where Jesus tells Mary, "Woman, here is your son." Then he turns to the mysterious Beloved Disciple (John?) and says: "Here is your mother." We're told at once that from that time on this disciple took Mary into his own house. In effect, Jesus is saying: Look after this woman; she is my mother. It's a powerful mo-ment, present only in John.

The dying words of Jesus are all taken from various moments in the Hebrew scriptures to make sure that readers understood that the execution of Jesus was a fulfillment of prophecy and thus part of a divine plan. But, again, the progress is swift from "I am thirsty" to "It is finished." And what precisely was finished? Jesus' life? His task? His sacrifice? Or are we to see yet another example of John's tendency to load words with multiple meanings?

Now we're told, only in John, that a body on a cross should not be left up during the Sabbath, so the body is hastily removed when Jesus expires. But first we get the piercing of the side and the telling detail that both blood and water flowed from the side of Jesus. The water, perhaps, links back to the opening scene with John the Baptist and continues the trope of water as something related to the eternal spirit.

Chapter 20 begins with Mary Magdalene coming to the tomb on the "first day of the week," Easter Sunday. Peter comes now, and others follow. But the body of Jesus is gone. Mary stands weeping outside the tomb, and when she stoops to look into the tomb itself, she sees two angels, who wonder why she is weeping. When she turns around, she sees Jesus, but she doesn't know him at first. When he speaks to her, she recognizes his voice and tries to fall upon him; but he warns her not to touch him yet, as he has to ascend to the Father. He asks her to inform the disciples that he is alive.

Then we cut quickly to the room where the disciples hide from the Jews, and Jesus comes to them and gives the traditional greeting: *shalom*. Peace be with you. Soon he breathes on them, bestowing the gift of the Holy Spirit.

We jump ahead eight days now, and Doubting Thomas sees the Lord, putting his finger in the nail holes and his hand in the spear wound (another scene unique to the Fourth Gospel). Jesus says: "Blessed are those who have not seen and yet have come to believe"—which echoes John's comment informing his readers that Jesus did not trust himself to people who believe because of signs. This must have been a powerful message to late first-century or early second-century followers of Jesus, the immediate audience of the Gospel writer. None of them would ever have the chance to see the Lord in person, to touch his side, so John is using these words to bolster them.

"Now Jesus did many other signs in the presence of the disciples, which are not written in this book," the author continues. A particular example follows in chapter 21. Peter and some friends are fishing in the Sea of Tiberias. Presumably they have fled Jerusalem and gone back to their old jobs as fishermen. But they are finding no fish. Jesus appears to them, but they don't recognize him. He tells them to cast their nets over the right side of the boat, and suddenly they catch a lot of fish (we are told the exact number): "So Simon Peter went aboard and hauled the net ashore, full of large fish, a hundred fifty-three of them." Again, the author knows that a good writer needs to offer exact details. It lends credibility. And this detail works exactly in this way.

These final scenes, especially those unfolding in the remainder of chapter 21, can seem oddly disjunctive, hastily assembled, so that many scholars believe the chapter was an appendix, perhaps added by some later editor. The final verse more or less says as much: "But there are also many other things that Jesus did; if every one of them were written down, I suppose that the world itself could not contain the books that would be written."

The Passion in John's Gospel narrative is, I suggest, rather underplayed as a physical or human drama but given a theological context that elevates Jesus to the level of the Cosmic Christ. He becomes here the Son of God, not so much the Son of Adam, although John would certainly have us understand that the incarnation implies a blending of God and man.

For me, one of the most intriguing aspects of resurrection (especially as portrayed with emphasis in John) is the fact that Jesus, as the risen Christ, is not immediately recognizable. This perhaps has something to do with the transmogrification from Jesus to Christ, the transformation of the earthly into a heavenly body. Jesus was a man. He was really a man, with recognizable features, a human body, although his spirit was singular and divine. As the risen Christ, he becomes a new thing in the world, difficult to recognize, even harder to acknowledge. He becomes water in the desert. He becomes *logos* itself, meaning transcendent, a shaping spirit. There is nothing literal here. It is all in the realm of the spirit now, with the divine spark igniting a conflagration that ultimately transforms matter itself into something harder, terrifying, and beautiful as well.

As a writer, John understood his tasks. He created an assembly of metaphors and tropes, threading them carefully through his narrative like beads on a string. He has a big story to tell: how the divine *logos* became Jesus the Christ and remains with his followers in the form of an equally divine spirit. He wants to understand this transformation in theological terms and to provide enough figurative language for this understanding to find embodiment. He has a uniquely elevated poetic manner, evident from the outset. And his accomplishment, as a writer, is both narrative and theological: he tells us a story with aplomb, yet he also deepens the narrative and carves its mythic dimensions, allowing its shape to resonate, its points to sing.

Working on
The Passion of Jesus of Nazareth

*"There's beggary in the love
that can be reckon'd"*

ELIZABETH COOK

When the composer Francis Grier approached me with a view to collaborating on a new Passion, it was clear that he wanted to do something other than set the Passion account of one of the four Gospels. He had specifically sought out a poet, and he intended to give me my head as a writer. In our early conversations we discussed how best to present the Passion story for a contemporary audience—an audience who could not necessarily be presumed to be familiar with either the events or the actors. Though we were aware our first audiences were likely to consist of those either devotionally or culturally familiar with the story, our aim was to reach beyond. We wanted to create a Passion that had the freshness and urgency of a story told for the first time.

While each of the Gospel writers wrote with knowledge of where his story was heading, the first actors in that story (arguably with the exception of Jesus) were living it in the dark, ignorant of outcomes and meanings. We wanted to create a Passion that would communicate not only the intense suffering of Jesus and his mother but also something of the experience of others caught up in the vortex of the events that led to the crucifixion of Jesus. Thus, we approached all of the characters as, to a greater or lesser degree, uncomprehending of the nature and meaning of the events that make up the story unfolding around them, which we know as the Passion.

In deciding not to use any single Gospel account as our source, we were diverging from the time-honored structure of a Passion oratorio; Bach, Scarlatti, Penderecki, Pärt, and Gubaidulina all wrote Passions that are settings of individual Gospels. Our decision was to use all four Gospels as our sources but not specifically to set the words of any. This decision made a quantitative difference (since there are many incidents that occur in only one Gospel) and also a qualitative one. By making all four Gospels our sources, we were already taking part in the tradition that follows from them—and in which we ourselves are participants. Inevitably, this tradition also became a source for our Passion.

As opposed to using a single, omniscient narrator—the evangelist of a single Gospel, for example—we chose to use multiple narrators, allowing participants in the story to take up the baton at the moment it passes to them. We planned a sequence of scenes with very different voices and viewpoints, each offering a different take on the events. In time, the partial or occluded understanding of these characters mirrored the inevitable incompleteness and downright distortion of our own comprehension. When the narrative lights on Bar-Abbas, for example, we wondered if he was astonished at his own unexpected liberation:

What could he (who is also named Jesus) know about Jesus of Nazareth? Might he be forgiven for thinking he was the center of the events that led to his reprieve? We also wanted children to be part of this account—partly for verisimilitude (there were surely a lot of children among the crowds in Jerusalem that day) but also because they occupy such a valued place in Jesus' ministry. They have a variety of roles in our Passion (including that of etymologists), and sometimes act as our narrators—indeed a child's voice opens the work. But they also contribute to the choruses and take part in the crowd's malicious taunting—when the adults are behaving like nasty children. Thus, we treat them as real children, not idealized little angels.

The crowd—often voiced by a congregation during Holy Thursday and Good Friday services—has a character of its own in our Passion. We wanted to show the dangerous dynamics of the mob, changing its mood at the slightest prompting and terrifyingly amplified or simplified by the number of people experiencing it. We show the crowd swerving from the idealization and enthusiasm of Palm Sunday to lethally malicious mockery during the trials, and finally to a kind of dissociated curiosity while watching the crucifixion. Both language and music show how easily delicacy and discernment may be extinguished by the dynamics of the mob and embody its terrifying violence—a violence and injury that touched our own natures. Francis Grier is a Kleinian psychoanalyst as well as a composer; my other work is in craniosacral therapy, which is concerned with emotions that are held in the body. Inevitably, therefore, our professional (as well as our direct and personal) experiences of the dynamics of emotions informed our discussions and our wish to show the full range and complexity of emotions that the participants might have lived through. The character of the crowd, which we came to regard as a many-headed monster, became essential to the momentum of our Passion.

Our decision to use multiple sources gave us freedom while imposing on us the need for choices of our own. In some ways the fact that I was not a biblical scholar was enabling. Emboldened by obliviousness to the difficulties and contradictions that would have been clear to an expert—and that soon became clear to me—I approached my commission with the confidence that at least the narrative sequence of events would be easy to establish, known to me through the Gospels themselves, the liturgy of Holy Week and Easter, through Bach's Passions, through Pasolini's film of Matthew's Gospel, through many works of visual art, and through some of the medieval mystery cycles. It was these last that encouraged me, with their freedom in telling the story. The way these dramas so evidently make use of the personalities, trades, and sense of humor of the communities that created them provided a liberating model. While the idea of following in the footsteps of the evangelists filled me, rightly I think, with a disabling alarm, I could more easily see myself as part of a continuing line of groups and individuals who had represented this story in order to experience it freshly in their own lives, retelling what will always need to be retold. *Yiimimangaliso*, a glorious South African version of the Chester mystery cycle that came to London in 2003, inspired and delighted us with its fullness and vitality, expressed in its dancing and polyglot singing (in English, Afrikaans, Xhosa, and Zulu). There was, we came to see, room for many voices.

Writing the libretto for this Passion was my first experience of creating a work in collaboration with a composer. Early on, Francis and I established a working relationship that was, in essence, an extended conversation: I would provide him with a draft of a scene, and he would respond to it musically (and often verbally). We never envisioned my writing all the words followed by his writing all the music. It was going to be a matter of my verbal language suggesting and provoking his musical language, with his music in turn provoking and suggesting new language. I soon learned that music could shift register and transform mood instantly, bestowing great freedom on the writer who works with a composer. Shifts of mode and mood, which would have been abrupt in words alone, became available to us. An almost magical freedom.

The work was not written in the order of the narrative: scenes and voices were fleshed out as they became imaginatively available to one or the other of us. Perhaps inevitably, it was easier for us to imagine a Peter or a Pilate than to approach the holiness of Jesus at the last supper or in the crucifixion. In thinking now about writing the words for this Passion, I am aware of being able to tell only half—if that —of the story. It is the music that lifts up the words and carries them into another dimension, enriching the story by adding an intense depth of feeling—as well as, at times, suggesting new ways to analyze and tell the story.

From the beginning Francis chose to echo Bach's compositional procedure of interweaving choruses, arias, and narratives. But as the story moves toward the crucifixion, these formal structures begin to break down under the dramatic pressure of events, until a more fragmented and chaotic oscillation between narration, violent crowd scenes, Jesus' words, and the chorus's reflections takes over. Finally, in the midst of this chaos, within and behind it, Francis chose to introduce a *chaconne*—a steady, repetitive musical structure much favored by Bach—thus establishing an underlying sense that some remorseless and inexorable pattern was being worked out. The sense that I (and others, surely) always have at the start of Holy Week—that there is now no way out except through the darkness of Good Friday—is wonderfully suggested in this musical structure, which counterpoints the distress and chaos of the drama. The great power of music suggests this directly without the intervention of conscious thought.

The process of working together as composer and poet resulted in a new understanding of a story we already knew well, with words and music coming together as *The Passion of Jesus of Nazareth*.

How to find a language for this work? We wanted our Passion to have a contemporary, twenty-first century voice. But we did not want this to be the only voice. In preparing to write the libretto, I read the Gospel accounts in as many different translations as I could, partly in an attempt to shake my imagination free of the complacencies of familiarity. W. L. Lorimer's *The New Testament in Scots* was particularly vital and fresh; reading it, one hears a real Scots voice speaking with urgency.

The narration and dramatic arias relate the events as they took place in the sequence made familiar through the Gospels. Here the use of a contemporary language (not always a high one) allows us in the twenty-first century to see ourselves as witnesses and active participants in the story. Additionally, the progress of the Christian tradition *through* time is represented by the means of varying the linguistic register. I had been brought up with the King James Version of the Bible and with Thomas Cranmer's *Book of Common Prayer*. I had also immersed myself for years in the work of the English metaphysical poets of the seventeenth century: as the register that has for so long carried and transmitted the story of the Passion for English speakers, it clearly needed a place in our telling. An even earlier stage in the tradition of Passion representation appears in the medieval lyric *Quanne hic se on rode* (When I see on the cross). This lyric speaks directly to us but in the language of earlier worshippers.

Though *The Passion of Jesus of Nazareth* lacks the voice of an evangelist (unless we count the Man in the Linen Cloth, whom some identify with Mark), it does include certain Gospel phrases that seemed to me to be indispensable. When Bach produced the score of his *Saint Matthew Passion*, he used red ink to distinguish the utterances of the evangelist (Matthew) from the rest of the text. For Bach those divine words required a special honoring. Though we do not mark them in red, we included certain Gospel phrases unaltered. Indeed our Passion's opening phrase, *There shall also be this,* echoes a verse from Matthew's story of the anointing of Jesus, *Verily I say unto you, wheresoever this gospel shall be preached in the whole world, there shall also this, that this woman hath done, be told for a memorial of her (26:13,* KJV). This verse is the most wonderful assertion of the persistence and indestructibility of a loving act; nothing can ever take it away or remove it from the story. I love this stubborn persistence. In my early work on the text I was looking for such moments of persistence, moments that push through the darkness of history and distance—like the white linen cloth left in the hands of the soldiers—moments where it seemed possible to hear and see and touch the original events. Such moments and details act like pins to hold the imagination in place.

The Aramaic words uttered by the dying Jesus, *Eloi, Eloi, lama sabacthani,* offer another such moment. The fact that they are recorded in Aramaic (like *Talitha cumi* in Mark 5:41, KJV) gives the impression of unmediated reportage. These Aramaic words are among the so-called seven last words of Jesus.

Tradition has made a narrative of the seven last words, memorably and eloquently set to music by Joseph Haydn. His sequencing of the words has an emotional logic to it. The piece begins by showing us Jesus continuing his ministry, even on the cross: interceding with the Father, comforting the repentant criminal, and arranging for the welfare of his mother and friend. The fourth word, *My God, my God, why hast thou forsaken me?* is the apex of the sequence, the moment of greatest darkness. A quotation from Psalm 22, it not only represents Jesus abandoned to the dark of the present but also as an observant Jew, so deeply versed in his own tradition's scriptures that they have become his own. The last three words in the sequence—*I thirst*; *It is finished;* and *Into your hands I commend my spirit*—trace a movement through the bodily suffering of Jesus to exhaustion, and finally to surrender to the will of God—again in the words of a psalm (31:5).

This sequence—often used for devotional meditation—was created by amalgamating the words of the four Gospels and ignoring the individual character of each one. Words one, two, and seven are taken from Luke—and do not occur in the other Gospels. Words three, five, and six appear only in John. Word four appears in Mark and Matthew.

In my decision to include all seven words in the traditional sequence I was of course enjoying a freedom that would not have been available had Francis chosen to set a single Gospel. Here I made a conscious decision to allow the tradition of liturgy and worship a place in the story. Whatever their claims to historical authenticity, these seven words have acquired the authority of original utterance by dint of devotional repetition. What we have made of the story has become part of the story.

Another part of the passion story I chose to include concerns the inscription on Jesus' cross. Though all the Gospels refer to it, we are told in the Gospel of John that Pilate *wrote a title. And the writing was, "Jesus of Nazareth, the King of the Jews." And it was written in Hebrew, and Greek, and Latin.* None of the Gospels gives us this inscription in the original languages; but I wanted us to be able to read the label at the foot of the cross. A literal-mindedness on my own part required that we hear each of the three languages, as well as their translation into English.

Apart from the seven last words (which are recast rather than quoted), I chose to use Jesus' sayings sparingly, omitting, for example, the pious prayer Matthew, Mark, and Luke tell us he uttered in the Garden of Gethsemane, *Father if thou be willing, remove this cup from me; nevertheless not my will, but thine, be done.* How can we know what he prayed in solitude, while his friends slept? Though these words, like the seven last words, have become part of the tradition, I felt that Jesus' aloneness in the garden would be better represented by watching him apart. Thus, we see him in the Garden but do not eavesdrop on his prayer. The chorale that follows observes:

> *He draws his cloak a little closer to keep out the chill,*
> *How the body recoils from even a little suffering.*

What we know is that the night was cold and how a human body would likely respond.

In telling other parts of the story three different though mutually informing modes of writing emerged—and in this Bach's Passions provided our model. The first mode was narrative: a single line of narration that is taken up by a variety of voices, either singly or severally. In places Francis made the decision for the narrator's voice to change almost mid-sentence, giving the impression of a collective retelling, of a crowd of individuals longing to come in with their piece to corroborate or extend what has already been said.

The second mode, which flows naturally from the first, is that of dramatic arias on the part of the participants: the narrative baton is passed on to an individual who was perhaps more closely involved in the events than the previous narrator, each one's piece of the story more personally expressive of the experience. An unusual feature of this Passion (which has positive practical implications for any performance) is that all the soloists are taken from the chorus—so that the "named parts" are also members of the community, which the chorus represents. The arias in the work may be dramatic, as is the case of Pilate's wife rushing in to tell her husband of her dream (a scene drawn from Matthew), or reflective, as is the case with Peter after the cockerel has crowed and he has remembered Jesus' words to him. The centurion's aria, near the end of the work, combines both modes, using elements from Mark and John: it tells the story in a very literal way, but then moves on to reflect and indeed make the most explicit statement of Jesus' divinity to come from a witness:

> So we broke the legs of two of the men
> But the middle one—Jesus—was dead already.
> Just to make sure I pushed in my lance to see if he'd
>   flinch.
> Not a twitch. Nothing.
> Just a trickle of blood
> and a trickle of water.
> I felt the earth shudder when the life left him.

I felt a tremor drive through my belly.
Something moved in me, went dark, went quiet.
Then when I touched his body with my lance
I knew that what they said of him was true.
He was the Son of God. He is.
And in my heart I worship him.

The third mode is that of the chorales and ariosos that punctuate the work and allow breathing spaces somewhat apart from the dramatic and historical narrative. For the structural placing of these, Bach was again our model: his *Saint Matthew Passion* is interspersed with moments, written by his librettist Picander—the pseudonym of Christian Friedrich Heinrici (1700–1764)—in which an eighteenth-century Lutheran Everyman can reflect on the present impact and meaning of the story being told. I listened again and again to two particular moments in the *Saint Matthew Passion*— "Erbarme mich" ("Have mercy on me") and "Ach Golgotha," soaking myself in the overflowing feeling of the words and music. However, the particular mode of self-address and Lutheran piety that was available to Bach and Picander is not our own. The chorales and ariosos in *The Passion of Jesus of Nazareth* have a different force and function: they allow moments of respite from the relentless forward movement of the narrative and a place for a voice from the twenty-first century. The inclusion of this voice is rather like the presence of the small donor figures painted, usually kneeling, by late medieval artists into large devotional scenes. Though a contemporary voice is implicit in the whole work, in both verbal and musical languages, it can be heard explicitly at these moments.

Our narrative begins and ends with the mortal, human body of Jesus. We wanted to present a fully *human* Jesus: a Jesus living

in a particular time and place; a man whose friends are recognizable from their local accent; and a devout Jew and a man who
walked on the earth (which the Buddhist monk Thich Nhat Hanh
regards as the true miracle in *The Long Road Turns to Joy*). The title,
The Passion of Jesus of Nazareth, flowed easily from the decision to
focus on the human Jesus. Though I considered the possibility
of opening with the transfiguration (following Matthew, who
seems to begin the passion story here), I realized that this would
be too glorious a start for the passion as we conceived it; such a
start would too thoroughly anticipate the resurrection. (In this
we differ from many other Passions, such as Sofia Gubaidulina's
Passion and Resurrection of Jesus Christ according to St. John, which
is composed from an Orthodox perspective and allows the resurrection to shine through the whole passion.) Thus, we begin
our Passion at Bethany, with the real, dusty, road-worn feet of
Jesus being anointed by Mary. And we conclude as the women
disciples, helped by Joseph of Arimathea—identified in this work
with the sorrowful rich man—and Nicodemus, wash the crucified body and bind it with linen and spices. This then was our
frame and our conception.

From the decision to focus on the human Jesus flowed other
decisions as well. Food is important in the Gospels, not just
spiritual food but also the greasy, nourishing stuff of broiled
fish and roast lamb. So many of the Gospel accounts of healing
are followed by the injunction to eat; in Luke's story of the encounter of the risen Christ at Emmaus, it is in the eating of the
meal that he is known. The last supper as we present it is a Seder
(and to signal this I used words close to those used in a formal,
contemporary Seder), and that Seder was also a *meal*, the last of
a great many that Jesus shared with his friends. For this reason

it is preceded by a chorus sung by the disciples, celebrating the physical life they have shared:

> *Small fires on the beaches:*
> *scent of driftwood burning to charcoal,*
> *fish roasting on hot stones;*
> *we tear the bread and press*
> *the hot cooked flesh in the soft crumb,*
> *licking our fingers clean*
> *of the salt taste of life and the sea.*
> *The many meals we have shared.*
> *The many good things to eat:*
> *butter and honey, figs and grapes,*
> *lamb and fish and bread and oil.*
> *We take good food in*
> *and speak good words out*
> *at the many meals we have shared.*

The Seder that is their last meal together is continuous with these experiences, but the chorale that announces it—set to shiveringly mystical music—is written in a more ceremonious, formal language. This music is repeated later from the side of the stage—an inspired musical suggestion that this meal, this ceremony, is being repeated and experienced by the many others who have gathered in Jerusalem for the Passover.

As a writer, often drawn to writing about the past, my perennial question is, What was it like? What was it like to have lived through these extraordinary events that have so changed the history of the world without knowing that they were not an end but a beginning? For many of those who took part in this story, the events would not even have been seen as remarkable: just another cult leader/

charismatic; just another crucifixion (there had recently been three thousand); just another day in Roman-occupied Judea. People then, as now, were more preoccupied with their own situations than events, however shocking, that did not concern them directly. As W. H. Auden observes in his poem "Musée de Beaux Arts," "About suffering they were never wrong, the old Masters."

While the decision not to limit ourselves to the account of a single Gospel (or even exclusively to the Gospel accounts) provided certain freedoms, the narrative that evolved needed coherence. Peter Brook wrote in *The Empty Space* that in theater "at every instant the practical question is an artistic one." Just so, when writing a Passion, every artistic/practical decision becomes, by implication, a theological one and, while neither Francis nor I would claim to be theologians, there is inevitably an implicit theology in the work. Jesus' washing of the disciples' feet occurs only in John's Gospel, where it takes place after a supper that is not a Passover meal. For John, Jesus *is* the Passover Lamb, and in this Gospel it is essential that the crucifixion take place on the day of preparation for the Passover, when lambs were being slaughtered for the Seder. Though I am familiar with a Holy Thursday liturgy that includes the foot washing before the Mass of the Last Supper, the implicit theology of our narrative dictated that we not include this lovely event—an event that in its tender physicality was in other ways so congruent to our conception. We did, however, choose to include characters that appear only in one Gospel. It is only in Matthew, for example, that Pilate's wife erupts into the story with the urgent message of her dream: an eruption so extraordinary that she was subsequently canonized for her recognition of Jesus' divinity (though of course such recognition is beyond anything in Matthew's account).

As well as Pilate's wife, there is Herod—to whom Jesus is sent only in Luke; Malchus, the soldier who lost an ear, is named only in John; and the unnamed man (sometimes identified with Mark himself and in whose Gospel he appears) literally gets caught up in the action of the arrest, dressed only in a linen cloth. All these characters are present in our Passion.

The list of our named parts includes Mary of Bethany, Judas, Jesus, Peter, the Man in the Linen Cloth, Malchus, Caiaphas, Pilate, Herod, Procula, Bar-Abbas, Veronica, Simon of Cyrene, Centurion, Joseph of Arimathea, and Nicodemus. The soldier who thought of the crown of thorns, with his Abu-Ghraib–style of inventiveness, has a solo aria celebrating his own cleverness. We also include the dialogue between Jesus and the two thieves crucified alongside him that appears only in Luke. Each of these is a character whose life has been marked by contact with Jesus, though in some cases it is the character's inability to see or be changed by this contact that is remarkable.

Our grounding the Passion in the physical body of Jesus is connected with a quality that the women in the story offer in particular ways. One short rhyme sung by the children makes the etymological connection between *mater* (mother) and *matter*. Though Jesus' mother, Mary, does not have a vocal role, she is in some sense present in the whole work. Mary of Bethany's opening aria, set to music that is marvelously sensual and celebratory, provides an affirmation of bodily life and love so encountered:

> *He saw what was lovely in me, not only*
> *my hips or my beautiful hair;*
> *he saw what was endless in me:*
> *Cool alabaster*

> *could not contain*
> *the all I would give him.*

Ideas of what is too much, what is endless, and what is beyond are present from the outset in this aria, which is all about breaking free and not being contained—the excess of her gift mirroring her profound experience of receiving love from Jesus. Mary of Bethany's love overflows; it is as unctuous as her ointment, and it is the love as much as the extravagantly spilling oil that so offends Judas. Her beautiful aria and lovely act are interrupted, shockingly pulled up short, and reined in by Judas. Her monosyllabic, *Then in walks Judas*, set by Francis Grier in a notably "unlovely" monotone, introduces language that is quantifying, literally calculating. Judas's voice is the voice of the spoiler, his envious destructiveness hiding behind a mask of rationality, *Have you any idea what oil like that costs?* Jesus replies in the language of more, of what may not be quantified: *More than you know.*

As suggested by the dialogue between Shakespeare's Antony and Cleopatra ("If it be love indeed, tell me how much. / There's beggary in the love that can be reckoned. / I'll set a bourn how far to be belov'd"), there is an overflowing language of love and self-offering, and a language of limitation and calculation that opposes it. The language and mindset of limitation simply does not comprehend the language or the experience of overflowing love.

The quality of overflowing—a quality of the menstruating, lactating female body, very much linked to the *matter* of the maternal body—is one that all the women in this Passion share. Mary of Bethany, Procula, and Veronica are alarming and powerful, possibly even embarrassing, presences because they do not keep within their bounds.

Pilate's wife seems to burst the banks of the narrative, breaking into Matthew's story, never to be forgotten. A name and biography have been credited to her retrospectively, picturing her as an aristocratic, fashion-conscious, Roman woman who is in every way out of her element in the Judea that her husband governed. By the time of the medieval mystery cycles she had become the rather comic figure of Dame Procula, a stock character in the story.[1] The fact that she erupts into Matthew's story may tell us something of his genius as a storyteller: the very *oddity* of a woman rushing in on her husband at work to tell him of her dream impresses the scene on our minds and of course suggests that the extraordinary nature of Jesus could affect and touch the psyches even of those he had not met. That she appears only in Matthew could suggest that this is a piece of the story that Matthew alone knew. But my motive in including this episode had less to do with its possible veracity than with an interest in the sheer *strangeness* of her presence in a story that gives particular value to her witness. She brings with her not only the unregulated world of the unconscious but also—with proleptic reference to the tradition she inspired—a whiff of the fashionable Roman world so different from the Judea in which the story takes place. She is also, conspicuously—even alarmingly—a woman in a very male judicial and martial environment.

The women included in our narrative—Mary of Bethany, Procula, and Veronica—share a quality of irregularity that the men around them—Judas, Pilate's soldiers, the guards forming a cordon by the roadside—want to restrain. These women offer

---

[1] Ann Wroe, *Pilate, The Biography of an Invented Man* (London: Vintage, 2000), 23–25, 37. See also Katie Normington, *Gender and Medieval Drama* (Cambridge: D. S. Brewer, 2006).

a level of experience that is both sensually aware and, partly as a consequence of this awareness, transgressive of boundaries. My decision to identify Veronica with the hemorrhaging woman of the Gospels was inspired by the soaked rags they have in common. The rags hold menstrual blood and the sweat of Jesus: body fluids that spill over and leave their mark. These, in turn, connect with the *excess* of Mary of Bethany's ointment, so that both women express spilling-over love, a love that offends through the generosity that refuses to keep within bounds.

Veronica's story, though non-scriptural, has occupied a central place in the tradition; her act of wiping Jesus' face is represented as the sixth station of the cross. The cloth she uses, the *sudarium,* has been variously construed as a holy relic or a perverse token of idolatry. Her aria is part reflection and part dramatic reenactment, sung in the present tense. The music that Francis wrote for her, a *mezzo*, is wild. Just as she breaks through the cordon of soldiers that holds back the crowd at the edge of the road, so does the music break out from the heavy, beautiful, and exhausted tones that evoke her, bleeding into something wildly ecstatic and almost hysterical:

> *Before they can stop me I break through*
> *the cordon of soldiers. I am quick.*
> *I wipe the sweat from his face with my cloth.*
> *The print of his face soaks into my cloth*
> *and See! the print of his face is still on it*
> *and I will never wash it.*

Again, there is something embarrassing and excessive in her feeling. She is like an adolescent girl sleeping with her idol's sweaty t-shirt under her pillow.

There are other events and characters that appear in only one Gospel that, through their very singularity, carry a particular weight of witness. The Man in the Linen Cloth, who appears only in Mark 14, is one such character: *And there followed him a certain young man, having a linen cloth cast about his naked body; and the young men laid hold on him; and he left the linen cloth, and fled from them naked.* This small story seems so incidental, so circumstantial, that we feel it surely must be true. This may be Mark's narrative genius at work. The presence of this episode is also a piece of pictorial genius: that flash of white linen in a night lit otherwise by torches (a scene from Rembrandt) somehow perfects the picture; it makes the scene an epiphany (in the Joycean sense). There is also a poetic anticipation of the linen cloths that will wrap Jesus' body—cloths that will also be unwound and found empty. All these factors weighed in my decision to include this incident. The short chorale that follows the dramatic narrative (taken over by the man himself) picks up on the poetic resonances:

> *He is not here.*
> *The chrysalis a paper shell,*
> *the winged moth has flown.*
> *The winding shroud empty,*
> *the beloved gone.*
> *Swaddled, bound, the wrapped creature*
> *is formed in dark*
> *then breaks out free.*

The figure of Malchus, the soldier who lost an ear, is named in John's Gospel—and only in John's Gospel (18:10–11). In the same place John names Simon Peter also (the Synoptic Gospels

speak only of "one of them"): *Then Simon Peter having a sword,
drew it, and smote the high priest's servant, and cut off his right ear. The
servant's name was Malchus.* In this passage the naming appears to
show inside knowledge on John's part. Indeed, later in the chapter there is reference to *that other disciple, which was known unto the
high priest.* The naming of Malchus—who makes only this one ap-
pearance in the Gospels—is one of those moments that one feels
must be true, because it serves no other purpose but to record
a truth. Since it was very much our intention to tell this story,
not from the single viewpoint of an evangelist but from multiple
and partial perspectives, this figure, whose own encounter with
Jesus must have been so painfully memorable, was an obvious
candidate for inclusion. Yet it is only in Luke's Gospel that the
soldier is healed (showing a physician's concern?). Luke, who like
John specifies that it is the *right* ear that is lost, situates the event
in a teaching to the disciples; *they said unto him,*

> "*Lord, shall we smite with the sword?*"
> *And one of them smote the servant of the high priest, and cut off
> his ear. And Jesus answered and said, "Suffer ye thus far." And he
> touched his ear, and healed him.* (22:49–51, KJV)

Malchus's experience of healing, like Procula's dream, is more
impressive because it is unexpected; it is not the experience of
the believer or even of one who wants to believe in Jesus' powers. In some ways it is as shocking and as sudden as—and far less
expected than—the initial wounding. The sheer strangeness of his
experience is wonderfully communicated by Francis Grier's setting of his narrative. Given to a counter-tenor voice, the strange
and haunting setting of Malchus's aria provides an extraordinary

moment of stillness in the middle of the very jarring evocation of the arrest:

> *At first I thought he was going to strike me*
> *then a different sword went through me—*
> *a piercing sweetness brought huge peace.*
> *He set his hand against my wound.*
> *In the midst of that uproar, huge peace.*
> *He healed my wound.*
> *My name is Malchus. I'm a soldier from Syria.*
> *I want to be part of this story.*

This little bit of autobiography is, of course, no more than a possibility, but it is a reminder of how many worlds and cultures converged in the Roman Empire, like the notion that the Simon who carries Jesus' cross is "a guest worker from Cyrene." Malchus's declaration, *I want to be part of this story*, expresses a sort of stubborn pride in the fact that nothing can ever remove him from this narrative or his role of witness. *There shall also be this. . . .*

The narrative of the trial is particularly confusing, since the four Gospel accounts differ in both time and sequence, while the exact nature of the charge against Jesus is still debated. Only in Mark does Jesus openly declare himself to be the Christ (in Luke, he responds with the more evasive, "You say so"), a blasphemy in the eyes of the religious hierarchy that leads the high priest to tear his garment in ritual repudiation. Only in Luke does Pilate send Jesus to Herod—a breather for Pilate or a piece of diplomatic networking—while in John's Gospel the painfully difficult process of Pilate's interrogation of Jesus is most fully set out. My abiding impression of John's Gospel is of a Jesus forever saying things that no one around him could understand, a Jesus in constant communication with the Father whose human interactions leave only puzzlement. John's account of the conversation between Pilate and Jesus is to me deeply mysterious. It is a conversation between two men who barely speak the same language. (Again we see the contrast between a language of measurement and calculation and a language that overflows and is transparent.) Pilate's questions and comments are full of incomprehension, and Jesus' replies help neither Pilate nor himself. There is a sense of Pilate struggling to find some chink in the armor, of his wanting to understand but of something obdurate and inexorable preventing his understanding. Francis Grier and I felt that Pilate undergoes a crucifixion of his own in his failure to do what he felt and knew to be right. From the moment that Jesus is sentenced—in the formulaic Latin words *Condemno, ibis in crucem*—Pilate is a broken man.

The encounter with Herod in the Gospel of Luke offered us an opportunity to present a man who is not faithful but superstitious (superstition being the travesty of faith), a man who is credulous and curious in an acquisitive way about the miracles Jesus is reputed to have performed but who entirely lacks the discernment to recognize who or what Jesus is. In the course of the aria I wrote for him he sings,

> *I hoped he might show me*
> *some pleasing miraculous tricks.*
> *Had he done so, he might have saved his neck.*
> *But the man was an imposter! He was nothing.*

Francis set this aria to a jazz saxophone, a surprising and funny moment that seems to me a musical equivalent to the comedy of a fat and overdressed Herod waddling onto the wagon stage in a mystery play.

Though there is no specific mention of children in the Gospel accounts of the Passion, the importance of children in Jesus' ministry made it imperative that they be represented in our telling. Musically, it was equally vital that the full range of human voices be heard. A newspaper photograph of children playing in the rubble after an earthquake in Colombia was on my desk when I pictured children playing in the dust by the road that leads to Golgotha. I wanted to convey something of the resilience of children, their ability to find an opportunity to play with the most uninviting materials and in the most inhospitable situations. Their play participates in the principle of creation, the *Maya* of Hindu theology. The actual children who sing in this work need to have fun. It is they who sing *"COCKADOODLE DO"* after Peter has denied his knowledge of Jesus. They sing it with exuberant relish and no more thought for Peter's feelings than the bird they represent.

A child's voice (this was Francis's decision) opens the Passion with the first (scriptural) words (*There shall also be this ...*)   a lovely soprano, the single chorister suggesting and invoking all the purity, perfection, and sweetness that is present in an idealized image of childhood. But the children in our Passion are also very real children, readily and unthinkingly joining in the taunts of the crowd, gleefully participating in its sadistic cruelty.

I have already mentioned that children are the etymologists of our Passion. (Perhaps etymology is something they learn at school!) They demonstrate that language itself—words as well as the Word—is source and substance in our story. The short etymological explications, which occur throughout the piece, are exercises in archeology, offering telescopic time travel. As we dig down into the earth to touch the roots of words, our own language with its dead metaphors is revitalized. In the words of the nineteenth-century etymologist Dean Trench, writing in *On the Study of Words,* "a single word is often a concentrated poem, a little grain of gold capable of being beaten out into a broad extent of gold-leaf." The first etymology that the children offer is in a chorus that occurs soon after Judas has interrupted Mary of Bethany's sumptuous aria. Judas's language, in opposition to hers, is all about cost, quantification. ("There's beggary in love that can be reckon'd," as we have seen.)

Somewhere behind this chorus was the memory of how, in Hans Christian Anderson's *The Snow Queen,* the boy Kay tries to say his prayers after the shard of ice has entered his heart, but all he can remember is his multiplication tables! The children show the link between calculation and stoniness:

> *Calculus: a little stone.*
> *Can you do your sums?*
> *Can you add, divide, subtract,*
> *do you know what each thing costs?*
> *Calculus: a little stone.*
> *Are you good at calculation?*

They are still playing with stones beside the road to Golgotha where, in the context of a playing rhyme, they give Latin for mother, *mater,* as the source of *matter:*

> *Have you got a little stone?*
> *You can throw it,*

you can count it,
you can put it in your pocket.
If you have a little water
we can make some mud to bake with.
Stone and water. Mater *matter.*
Let's play. Play with me!
What game shall we play?

Stone, earth, and water: the basic materials of the landscape and elements of creation.

The most extended passage of the children's etymology pointedly occurs at the time of the crucifixion. After a brief, and musically very moving, chorus

(She can only endure.
She can only bear.
She will not shelter from the pain.
But a mother should not live longer than her son.)

there follows this chorus, which "beats out" (to use Trench's phrase) the layers of meaning contained in the word *passion*—a word that we in our own time so limit and impoverish by confining it to sexual passion:

the Latin patior: *to suffer or bear,*
patience: the virtue of bearing,
passive: to denote that which bears,
patent: for that which lies open
and *passion:* a surrender to bearing
so great it is stronger than action.

Her Passion—His Passion—
in which he lies open
to all the weight of earth and heaven.

The intellectuality of this chorus, at the moment of such extreme suffering (the crux of the cross), evokes the kind of defensive reflex commonly triggered in a mind confronted by what cannot be borne. It also, I hope, rescues the word *passion* from its current debasement.

This defensive reflex, this turning away from what cannot be contemplated in any sustained way, was part of my own experience in working on *The Passion of Jesus of Nazareth*. In describing the rational and creative decisions made in the process of writing this work thus far, I have avoided the central question of how it was also a devotional experience. But in fact, many of the aesthetic decisions I made also involved devotional decisions. The decision *not* to assign additional words to Jesus or his mother at a number of important moments—despite a long tradition of doing so in medieval poetry and drama—stemmed from my sense of the impertinence of such prosopopoeia. What should be limitless in them would be limited, I felt, by assigning more words. To characterize Mary and Jesus in this way would be to make them too small and to diminish the potential fullness of meaning that I hoped listeners might experience at crucial moments. The two scenes that I found most daunting were the last supper and the crucifixion. Each, I thought, could be approached only by attending to the recorded specifics of the events. In order to write them I needed to undertake something similar to the practice of Ignatian meditation, imagining every detail as fully as I was able. Yet the mind cannot stay with such suffering for very long. (It is the great gift of Mary, Jesus' mother, that she can and does.) I found myself imagining how the defenses of others who were present would have been aroused. I imagined, for example, the black humor of soldiers for whom this kind of violence was part of their everyday work and thus gave them a rhyme to which they hammer in the three nails—a rhyme that inadvertently evokes the Father, the Mother, and the Holy Spirit.

I once had the idea of including a great many non-scriptural quotations in our Passion—lines from George Herbert, say, or from Julian of Norwich, or the church fathers—binding them in a patchwork of the tradition. In the end, however, I used only one such quotation: the medieval lyric *Quanne hic se on rode,* which Benjamin Britten also set in his composition *Sacred and Profane* (1974–75). The simplicity and directness of this lyric response is to me the essence of what the Hindus call *bhakti*—the approach to the divine through love.

Quanne hic se on rode	When I see on the cross
Ihesu mi lemman	Jesus my beloved
An besiden him stonden	and beside him standing
Marie and Iohan	Mary and John
and his rig isuongen	and his back flogged
and his side ustungen	and his side pierced
for the luve of man;	for the love of man;
wel ou hic to wepen	well ought I to weep
and sinnes forleten	and [my] sins forsake
yif hic of luve can	if I know of love
yif hic of luve can	if I know of love
yif hic of luve can.	if I know of love.

The inclusion of this lyric here, at the moment of the crucifixion, connects us, the twenty-first-century witnesses, to those who have contemplated this scene in the past. This single medieval lyric stands for two millennia of contemplation.

In keeping with our decision to present a fully human Jesus, the narrative itself contains no glancing forward to Easter Day. It adheres closely to the events leading up to the crucifixion and then to the crucifixion itself, without offering any consolatory promise of the resurrection. There are, however, moments when the language and imagery may hint at the larger, eschatological, picture. The final chorale, in particular, contains intimations of what is to come:

> *Quiet of the garden,*
> *the dark earth waits and every stalk*
> *stands to attention.*
> *Cups of flowers the light pressed open*
> *scatter their petals,*
> *litter the ground, broken.*

Czeslaw Milosz has written, "To remain aware of the weight of fact without yielding to the temptation to become only a reporter is one of the most difficult puzzles confronting a practitioner of poetry."[2] I wanted to find a language that would balance a scrupulous adherence to reported events with a sense—as subtle as the bloom on grapes—of what those events might mean, without imposing a heavy symbolism that would nudge the hearer toward interpretation. Music can take language further than it

---

[2] Czeslaw Milosz, *New and Collected Poems 1931–2001* (New York: Ecco, 2001), xxi.

can take itself. Francis Grier's setting of the concluding chorale repeats the last word, "broken," again and again by a wide range of voices—dissonant, plaintive, tentative, and flat voices—turning it over and over, examined, gutted, and exhausted. The word points to the breaking of the day and to the breaking of bread by which the risen Christ is known at Emmaus. It leaves us with the broken body of Jesus.

Contributors

Julia Alvarez is a poet, novelist, and essayist. Born in the Dominican Republic, the setting of many of her stories, she now lives and writes in Middlebury, Vermont. She is the author of *The Woman I Kept to Myself: Poems* (2004), *Before We Were Free* (2002), *A Cafecito Story* (2001), *In the Name of Salome* (2000), *The Secret Footprints* (2000), *Something to Declare: Essays* (1998), *Yo!* (1997), *Homecoming: New and Collected Poems* (1996), *The Other Side: El Otro Lado* (1996), *In the Time of the Butterflies* (1994), *How the Garcia Girls Lost their Accents* (1990), and *Homecoming* (1984). In July 2014 she received the National Medal of Arts "for her extraordinary storytelling."

Elizabeth Cook's writing has taken many forms. Her academic work includes *Seeing Through Words* (1986) and *John Keats: The Major Works* (1996). Her novel *Achilles* (2003) received wide praise, as did *Bowl* (2006), a collection of poems. She has published short fiction and poetry in numerous venues; she has also written for both television and theater. Cook wrote the libretto for Francis Grier's *The Passion of Jesus of Nazareth* (2006), a collaborative project commissioned by the BBC.

John Elder, professor emeritus of English at Middlebury College, is an essayist whose works include *Spirit and Nature: Why the Environment Is a Religious Issue—An Interfaith Dialogue* (with Stephen Rockefeller, 1992), *Following the Brush* (1993), *Reading the Mountains of Home* (1999), *The Frog Run: Words and Wilderness in the Vermont Woods* (2002), and *Pilgrimage to Vallombrosa* (2012).

Jay Parini is the D. E. Axinn Professor of English and Creative Writing at Middlebury College. Among his many books and essays are *The Last Station: A Novel of Tolstoy's Last Year* (1990), *John Steinbeck: A Biography* (1995), *Robert Frost: A Life* (1999), and most recently *Jesus: The Human Face of God* (2013). He and his wife, Devon Jersild, are currently working on a screenplay based on his novel *The Passage of H. M.: A Novel of Herman Melville* (2010). Parini is also completing a new critical biography of Gore Vidal.

Stephanie Saldaña is the author of the memoir *The Bread of Angels* (2010) and the forthcoming book *The Country Between* (2015). She teaches literature and is director of First Year Seminar at Al-Quds Bard College, a partnership between Bard College in Annandale, New York, and Al-Quds University in the West Bank. She lives with her family in Jerusalem.

Oliver Larry Yarbrough is the Tillinghast Professor of Religion and director of the Scott Center for Spiritual and Religious Life at Middlebury College in Middlebury, Vermont. His teaching and research focus on biblical studies and the origins of Judaism and Christianity; he has recently edited *Engaging the Passion*, a collection of essays that examines the Passion texts and their treatment in liturgy, music, art, literature, film, theology, and ethics. Yarbrough is also a priest in the Episcopal Diocese of Vermont.